D1524982

The Most Epic Football Stories for Kids

Discover incredible real-life stories from football legends & encourage young athletes to excel both on and off the field!

By

W. Bo Cricklewood

W. Bo Cricklewood

"To be successful at anything, the truth is you don't have to be special. You just have to be what most people aren't: consistent, determined and willing to work for it."

- Tom Brady

W. Bo Cricklewood

Table of Contents

W. Bo Cricklewood

Introduction

Welcome to the thrilling world of football, where legends are born and dreams come true! Imagine yourself in a packed stadium, the roar of the crowd washing over you like a tidal wave of excitement. Can you feel the energy? That's the magic of football, and it's waiting for you right here in these pages.

Get ready to meet some of the most incredible athletes to ever step onto the field. We're talking about superstar quarterbacks like Tom Brady, who went from being picked last to becoming the greatest of all time. And running backs like Walter Payton, who ran circles around defenders and into the history books.

But here's the thing – these football heroes weren't born with superpowers. They were once kids just like you, with big dreams and the determination to make them happen. They faced challenges, doubts, and setbacks, but they never gave up. And that's what makes their stories so amazing.

As you read about these legends, you'll discover that greatness isn't just for the pros. It's for anyone who's willing to work hard and believe in themselves. That includes you! So, are you ready to be inspired? To learn how to tackle your own challenges and score big in life?

Get ready to laugh, cheer, and maybe even shed a tear or two as you dive into these epic football tales. Who knows? You might just find the motivation to start writing your own legendary story. So, what are you waiting for? Turn the page and let the adventure begin!

Chapter 1: The GOAT: Tom Brady's Journey from Pick #199 to 7 Super Bowl Rings

From Underdog to Unstoppable

In the world of sports, we often hear the tale of the underdog—the underestimated hero who rises up against the odds. Few stories capture this spirit quite like that of Tom Brady, a name now synonymous with greatness in football. Picture yourself as a teenager, juggling the pressures of school, friendships, and sports. For Brady, this was the backdrop for his extraordinary journey, a journey that would eventually see him become one of the most celebrated quarterbacks in NFL history.

Growing up in San Mateo, California, Brady discovered his love for football early on. But it wasn't just a hobby; it was a passion that ran deep. He faced challenges just like any aspiring athlete, often competing against friends who were just as devoted but taller, stronger, and faster. Brady wasn't the star player in high school; he had to put in extra effort just to earn a spot on the team. As he donned his high school colors, self-doubt often overshadowed the bright stadium lights.

Brady's high school experience wasn't marked by championships or awards. Instead, it was filled with countless hours of practice, sweat in the weight room, and an unyielding voice inside him urging him to keep going. Playing for Junípero Serra High School, he frequently found himself overshadowed by peers who would go on to major universities. Yet, it was in this competitive environment that Brady sharpened his skills, proving that hard work and determination could help him keep pace.

As time passed, the world of college football beckoned. Brady earned a spot at the University of Michigan, but it was far from a storybook experience. With experienced players ahead of him, he often found himself on the sidelines, observing and learning while he waited for his chance to shine. This was a time that tested his resolve. Coaches scrutinized his every move, and fans wondered if he had what it took to lead a team. But through it all, Brady's determination never wavered.

The college experience pushed him to improve. He studied the game with a keen eye, learning from every mistake and celebrating even the smallest victories. He practiced relentlessly, staying late to perfect his throws. Those solitary hours on the field helped him develop a deep bond with his craft and a work ethic that would define his career. Brady's rise wasn't instantaneous; it was a long path filled with challenges. Each setback became a lesson, teaching him that true greatness requires perseverance.

When the NFL Draft day rolled around in 2000, the air was thick with anticipation. Family, friends, and hopeful athletes gathered around screens, anxiously waiting for their names to be called. For Brady, the tension was intense. Despite his college experience, he still felt like an underdog. When the first round ended and his name wasn't called, hope began to fade. Then, the number 199 flashed on the screen—he had been selected by the New England Patriots. What should have been a moment of joy was tinged with disbelief. How could a quarterback from Michigan, who spent so much time on the bench, be picked so late?

To many, Brady was just another face in a crowd of hopefuls, easily forgotten. But deep inside, he felt a spark of motivation. The world had underestimated him, and he was determined to prove them wrong. The skepticism he faced fueled his drive, igniting an unquenchable thirst to carve out his legacy. This moment solidified his identity as the ultimate underdog—an identity he would embrace wholeheartedly.

As Brady stepped into the Patriots' training camp, the pressure increased. Surrounded by seasoned pros, every day presented new challenges. Coaches watched closely, analyzing every throw and decision. He struggled to adapt to the fast-paced game, battling doubts that crept in. Would he ever meet expectations? Or would he slip into obscurity, a name lost among forgotten players?

This time was anything but glamorous. Brady faced long days filled with grueling practices that tested both his physical and mental strength. As he fought for the starting quarterback position, he faced setbacks that would have discouraged many. Missed throws, failed drills, and moments of doubt threatened to derail his dreams. But he learned an invaluable lesson: every failure was a chance to grow.

Brady's resilience shone through as he tackled challenges head-on. He sought guidance from coaches, watched game tapes late into the night, and spent countless hours on the practice field, determined to improve. Each obstacle only strengthened his resolve. While others saw problems, he viewed them as stepping stones to success. He understood that nothing worth achieving comes easy.

It was during this time that his leadership began to take shape. Even as a rookie, he was willing to put in the extra effort to earn the respect of his teammates. He approached every practice with the mindset of a champion, encouraging those around him to elevate their game. He knew that a team is only as strong as its weakest link, and he was committed to lifting everyone.

Brady's relentless work ethic and determination eventually paid off. As the season went on, he found himself in a fierce competition for the starting quarterback position. Facing both talented and experienced players, his confidence grew with every practice and game. He learned to drown out the critics and remind himself that he belonged on that field.

The pivotal moment came when an injury to the starting quarterback opened the door for Brady. He grabbed that opportunity with both hands, stepping onto the field like he

had been waiting for this moment his whole
life. The stadium erupted, and for the first
time, the world was about to see the
transformation of an underdog into an
unstoppable force.

As he took charge of the huddle,
Brady's nerves were replaced by fierce
determination. This was his moment to show
that he belonged among the best. With each
snap, he gained confidence, reading defenses,
executing plays, and making decisions that
highlighted his growing understanding of the
game. The very essence of being
underestimated drove his performance.

Brady's journey wasn't just about
personal achievement; it was a victory over
adversity. It symbolized the power of believing
in oneself, a theme that resonates with anyone
who has ever felt overlooked. For young
readers, Brady's story is a powerful reminder
that greatness can come from the most
unexpected places. It encourages them to trust
in their abilities, keep working hard, and never
let others' opinions dictate their paths.

As the season unfolded, Brady
continued to defy expectations. What began as
a desperate quest for recognition blossomed
into a remarkable career characterized by
determination, resilience, and unyielding
passion. Every touchdown he threw and each
game he won served as proof of the strength

that comes from self-belief. Tom Brady's journey from being the 199th pick to a force to be reckoned with is an inspiring story, urging young readers to embrace their challenges and rise above.

The road ahead wouldn't be easy, and the challenges would only grow tougher. But as Brady reflected on his beginnings—from the sidelines of high school fields to the dazzling lights of the NFL—he realized that his journey was just getting started. It was a path fueled by relentless drive, commitment, and the courage to dream big. This lesson would resonate for years to come, reminding us that the most incredible stories often begin with an underdog.

The Power of Perseverance

Football is much like life; it's a grand stage where the script often remains unwritten. Tom Brady's path to becoming one of the greatest quarterbacks wasn't just about his natural talent; it was deeply rooted in something more powerful: a strong commitment to perseverance. This relentless work ethic, his desire for excellence, and the determination to improve every single day became the secret ingredient to his amazing success.

When we take a closer look at the daily routines and habits that shaped Brady's life, a clear pattern starts to emerge. It's not just about the excitement of game day, the cheers from the fans, or the headlines praising him as a champion. It's about the countless hours he poured into his training, often waking up before dawn while many were still snoozing in their beds. Brady was already up, tying his cleats and hitting the gym. This dedication didn't happen overnight; it was built step by step, day by day, as he worked hard to improve his skills.

Brady's training was legendary. Those early mornings turned into marathon sessions, where he felt a weight lift off his shoulders with each rep he completed. His workouts were carefully planned, with every drill serving a purpose, enhancing not just his physical strength but also his mental sharpness. The drive to leave no stone unturned pushed him to reach for greatness, always striving for perfection in everything he did.

He also dedicated countless hours to studying film, carefully analyzing not only his own performances but those of his opponents too. Brady became a true student of the game, combing through footage, breaking down plays, and anticipating defensive moves. This showed his incredible commitment to self-improvement—understanding that in a game as dynamic as football, staying ahead meant being willing to learn and adapt constantly.

But perseverance is more than just a set of routines. It's also about having the courage to face setbacks head-on. Brady's journey wasn't without its challenges—he encountered injuries and losses that could have easily crushed a less determined athlete. His rookie year was a rollercoaster filled with lessons that tested his resilience. These ups and downs were not just obstacles; they were opportunities for growth, a theme that would resonate throughout his career.

Think about the injuries that sidelined him. Each time he had to step back from the game, it would have been easy to give in to frustration or doubt. Instead, Brady used these moments as chances for self-reflection. He saw every setback as an opportunity to learn something new. The long hours spent recovering and the tough rehabilitation sessions weren't just hurdles; they were crucial steps on his journey to improvement. He realized that setbacks could either mean the end of the road or simply a detour toward even greater destinations.

Then there were the losses, which can haunt any athlete but became turning points for Brady. Early in his career, he experienced moments that could have left him shaken—games that slipped away, chances lost. While others may have retreated into despair, Brady chose to reflect on what had gone wrong, how he could improve, and how to come back stronger. Each defeat helped shape his character, deepening his resolve and igniting a fire within him to be better.

It's often said that true character isn't built in times of comfort but in moments of struggle. Brady truly embodies this idea. His experiences showed him that the road to success is often lined with challenges, and how one responds to those challenges reveals a lot about their character. When faced with difficulties, he didn't just survive; he thrived. He learned how to turn adversity into an advantage, channeling his frustrations into focused efforts for improvement.

The lessons Brady learned through perseverance didn't just sharpen his skills on the field; they became part of his broader philosophy in life. This lesson goes beyond sports, resonating with the dreams and aspirations of many. Young athletes, students, or anyone striving for success can find inspiration in Brady's unwavering dedication to personal growth.

Throughout his career, Brady often emphasized the importance of self-reflection as a key part of the journey toward success. He encourages a mindset that embraces challenges as vital components of the process. What does perseverance mean to you? How do you handle setbacks? These questions invite readers to reflect on their own journeys, encouraging them to take a page from Brady's playbook and realize that challenges can lead to remarkable growth.

For young readers, the message is clear: face your challenges and commit to improving yourself. Whether it's on the field or in any part of life, remember that perseverance isn't just about the end goal; it's about the journey. Every challenge is an opportunity waiting to be grabbed, and each setback can be the very thing that propels you forward.

Brady's relentless pursuit of improvement reminds us that success isn't a straight path; it's a winding road filled with twists, turns, and unexpected bumps. While it's easy to celebrate victories, true champions recognize the lessons learned from their struggles. They appreciate the insights gained through hard times and understand that every challenging moment shapes who they are.

So, as we explore the power of perseverance through Brady's journey, it's clear that his story is more than just about football. It's a universal tale of resilience and growth that inspires us all to push through challenges, maintain a strong work ethic, and strive for improvement in our own lives. The world may sometimes feel overwhelming, but with determination, we can carve our paths and reach our dreams.

By embracing the lessons of perseverance, we not only honor Brady's journey but also empower ourselves to face our challenges with courage, nurturing a mindset that values growth, resilience, and the belief that anything is achievable if we are willing to put in the effort. Through consistent hard work and a commitment to self-improvement, we too can rise to meet the expectations we set for ourselves, just as Brady did throughout his remarkable career.

Leadership on and off the Field

When we think about the legendary figures in sports, it's easy to get caught up in the numbers, the records, and the incredible plays that shape their careers. However, there's a richer story behind the stats, one that highlights the true essence of leadership—a crucial quality that not only drives athletes to achieve greatness but also lifts up everyone around them. Tom Brady, a name that stands out in the world of football, is a shining example of this kind of leadership. His journey from a rookie quarterback eager to prove himself to a seasoned veteran who inspires teammates and fans alike is a story worth sharing.

At the heart of effective leadership is the ability to connect with others. It's about bringing people together for a shared goal, turning a group of players into a tight-knit team. Brady possesses a unique gift for building trust and friendship within his squads. Many of his teammates remember how just his presence in the locker room could change the mood from anxious to excited and determined. This special energy is what has made him a lasting icon in sports, moving beyond his impressive skills to become a true leader.

Brady's leadership style is rich and varied. He combines charm, an unyielding work ethic, and a deep knowledge of the game. His teammates often speak of how he can rally them during crucial moments, especially when the stakes are high. Picture this: the game is on the line, the clock is ticking down, and the opposing team is closing in. The weight of expectation hangs heavy in the air. In those intense moments, Brady steps up—not just with a strategy, but with a message that strikes a chord: "We can do this. Together."

Through conversations with fellow players and coaches, it's clear that Brady has a special talent for transforming nerves into action. His calm presence amid the chaos serves as a guiding light for those around him. Whether it's a reassuring touch or an impassioned call to action, he knows how to instill confidence in his teammates when they need it the most. His words go beyond simple motivation; they are a rallying cry, reminding everyone that they are part of something bigger. This became particularly evident during critical playoff moments when a single drive could determine the outcome of the entire season.

Leadership, however, isn't limited to the field. The lessons Brady learned under pressure carry over into his personal life and community involvement. While his athletic achievements are certainly impressive, it's his dedication to making a positive impact that truly highlights his character. Brady doesn't shy away from advocating for causes he believes in, embracing the idea that success should be meaningful and not just about personal gain. His charitable work spans various areas, including health initiatives and educational support, showing a deep understanding of the responsibilities that come with fame.

A shining example of his commitment to the community happened during his time with the New England Patriots. After Hurricane Katrina wreaked havoc, Brady teamed up with other athletes to raise funds for those affected. His involvement went beyond simply writing a check; he actively participated in campaigns, using his fame to gather support. In a time when many athletes focus solely on their own lives, Brady's choice to step up for a cause larger than himself embodies what it means to be a true leader.

Brady's charitable efforts have sparked inspiration in many young athletes, encouraging them to look beyond their own achievements. By sharing these stories, he motivates the next generation to consider how they can use their talents to help others. His advocacy serves as a reminder that the road to greatness is not just about personal glory, but also about contributing to the community. In a world where young people often seek role models, Brady offers a powerful narrative that connects athletic excellence with a genuine commitment to service.

As we reflect on Brady's journey, the theme of empowerment stands out. He represents the belief that anyone can be a leader in their own way. Leadership isn't always about being the captain or the loudest voice in the room. It can show itself in various forms—through kindness, support, or simply by setting an example of hard work and determination. Brady's unyielding drive to improve and his eagerness to uplift others prove that leadership is more about mindset than titles.

Brady's influence resonates on and off the field. Young readers can draw motivation from his story, realizing that the qualities that define great leaders are within their reach. It's about being honest, dependable, and inspiring others to reach for their best. The truth is that anyone can lead—whether in sports, at school, or within their communities. By encouraging young people to embrace these values, we nurture a future generation of leaders ready to make a difference.

At the core of Brady's legacy is a powerful message: hard work, resilience, and leadership can change lives—not just in sports, but in every aspect of life. His experiences inspire young readers to chase their dreams while uplifting those around them. As they pursue their goals, they should remember that true greatness comes from achieving personal success while also fostering teamwork and collaboration.

Ultimately, the story of leadership and community is a profound one, reminding us that we are all connected. As we follow our passions and aim to make an impact, we should hold onto the lessons from leaders like Brady. By creating a culture of support, accountability, and empowerment, we can lift each other up, much like Brady has throughout his career. Each time we lend a hand, offer encouragement, or celebrate our victories together, we help create a legacy of leadership that extends far beyond the football field.

As young readers reflect on Brady's journey, they are invited to think about how they can embody these qualities in their own lives. It's a call to recognize their unique strengths, advocate for change, and lead by example. After all, every great leader starts somewhere, and by following in the footsteps of those who inspire us, we can pave our paths to greatness—not just for ourselves, but also for those who come after us. The legacy of leadership is one of empowerment, and it's a legacy that begins with each of us.

W. Bo Cricklewood

Chapter 2: Never Give Up: Kurt Warner's Path from Grocery Store to Super Bowl MVP

A Rocky Road to the NFL

Kurt Warner's journey starts not on the bright, flashy fields of the NFL, but in the welcoming streets of Cedar Rapids, Iowa. Picture a sunset casting a warm glow over cozy homes, with kids laughing and tossing a football around the neighborhood. This was where Warner grew up, dreaming big amid the joy of friends and the cheers of family. For Kurt, football was more than just a game; it was a passion that bubbled inside him, ready to explode with excitement. He could often be found perfecting his throws with pals or glued to the TV on weekends, dreaming of the day he would step onto that field himself.

His family played a huge role in nurturing his love for the game. Kurt often reminisced about his dad taking him to local high school games, where he watched in awe as players raced across the field, and the crowd erupted with excitement. His family was his biggest cheerleading squad, celebrating every game, no matter how big or small. Every touchdown he scored in Pop Warner football sparked a flame in his heart, fueling his hopes of one day making it to the NFL. He dedicated himself to practice, throwing pass after pass, visualizing himself as the next football superstar. But despite his talent, recognition didn't come as quickly as he'd hoped.

High school brought its own challenges. While he showed promise, Warner wasn't the star player everyone anticipated. He played, but he wasn't exactly the one everyone was talking about. While his teammates received scholarship offers left and right, Kurt felt like he was in the background, overlooked and undervalued. During this time, he learned an important lesson about hard work and dedication: just because the spotlight isn't on you doesn't mean you can't shine.

Rather than sulking, he focused on improving his skills, practicing tirelessly day after day while the cheers from the stands faded into quiet whispers.

When high school ended, Kurt took a big step into the world of college football. He aimed for the University of Northern Iowa, hoping to prove himself and step up his game. However, college life wasn't the glamorous experience he had imagined. Moving to a new place, he felt a mix of excitement and nerves, only to discover that every other player was just as eager to snag the starting quarterback position. Kurt found himself back at square one, training hard while the fierce competition made his dreams feel like they were slipping away.

As the years went by, doubts began to creep in. After facing some setbacks, including injuries and inconsistent performances, the NFL felt more like a distant dream. It's easy to picture Kurt behind the scenes, balancing studies and football while working at a grocery store to make ends meet. Many young dreamers can relate to this part of his life. Imagine starting your day to the sounds of shopping carts and cash registers, trading in the thrill of football for scanning groceries and bagging apples. Warner often shared that the grocery store wasn't just a job for him; it became a symbol of his life—a place where he felt stuck but still determined to reach for something more.

His daily grind included everything from stocking shelves to ringing up customers. Amidst the hustle, he found little pockets of time to dream. Picture him pushing carts filled with groceries while imagining throwing a perfect pass in the NFL or hearing the roar of a packed stadium. His coworkers were friendly, often teasing him about his lofty dreams, but there was a mutual respect beneath the playful banter. They recognized he was chasing something many wouldn't even dare to pursue, and for Kurt, that belief—even from those who saw him at his most ordinary—became a source of strength.

Despite the fatigue from working nights and weekends, he squeezed in training whenever he could, determined to keep the flame of football alive in his heart. He never allowed that spark of passion to die, even when things felt tough. However, it wasn't all smooth sailing. There were days filled with frustration, nights of self-doubt, and moments when he considered giving up. The dreams he carried sometimes felt like heavy weights, but every setback taught him something important: the power of perseverance in tough times.

Those days spent stocking shelves and missing chances weren't in vain; they were building blocks that helped him develop a resilient spirit. He learned how to get back up after every fall, realizing that the road to achieving his dreams wouldn't always be easy. There's something incredibly raw about discovering that life's hardest challenges can become our greatest teachers.

Even when multiple teams overlooked him and he faced rejection, Kurt refused to give up on his dreams. The NFL was a world where dreams could either take flight or crash down hard, but he was determined to keep fighting. With a heart full of passion and a strong belief in himself, Warner decided he wouldn't be defined by his job at the grocery store or the hurdles he faced in college. Instead, he aimed to rise above it all, showing that sometimes the most incredible success stories begin in the most unassuming places.

While others might have settled for less, Kurt Warner held onto the idea that every setback was just a setup for an amazing comeback. As he worked those grocery shifts, his dreams loomed larger on the horizon, pushing him to keep moving forward. Little did he realize, the path ahead would be nothing short of extraordinary, filled with the kind of twists and turns that make for an unforgettable story. The journey to the NFL was rocky, but every bump along the way only added to the incredible tale of a man who would soon become a household name and a

Super Bowl MVP, inspiring countless generations to chase their dreams.

Seizing the Moment

Every great story has that pivotal moment, the instant when everything changes and the unexpected bursts forth. For Kurt Warner, this moment was shaped by his unwavering love for football, all while juggling a mundane grocery store job that felt more like a burden than a stepping stone. Even surrounded by shelves of soup cans and cereal boxes, his heart soared with dreams of touchdowns and roaring crowds. The contrast between his everyday life and his relentless ambition painted a powerful picture—a story of resilience that resonates with countless dreamers who refuse to let their circumstances stifle their aspirations.

To picture Kurt in the grocery store is to see someone out of sync with his environment, almost like a lion among sheep. Each day, he donned his work apron and faced the monotonous tasks of stocking shelves, ringing up customers, and maneuvering through aisles bursting with bright packaging. Yet, behind the scenes of that grocery store, a fire burned just beneath the surface. Whenever he found a spare moment, Kurt transformed the break room into his personal gym. He wasn't just pushing shopping carts; he was pushing himself, lifting weights of ambition that felt heavier than any grocery load.

Kurt's routine evolved into a powerful ritual that went beyond his job. He rose early, driven not just by the demands of his shifts but by the excitement of training. His backyard turned into an impromptu practice field, where a basketball hoop served as the perfect target for his throws. Each pass he launched felt like a declaration—a promise to the universe that he was more than the limitations of his current situation. Picture him there, sweat glistening on his forehead, determination carved into his features, pouring all his energy into every throw as if each one brought him closer to his dreams.

Those workouts were intense. He practiced footwork, agility drills, and those perfect spirals that he hoped would one day land him in the NFL. There was something contagious about Kurt's dedication. He often invited friends for scrimmages, turning friendly games into high-energy sessions that sharpened his skills and fueled his competitive spirit. As he threw the ball, he imagined defenders closing in and the electrifying atmosphere of a game-winning drive. Each practice was more than just a workout; it was a way to keep the belief in a dream that felt both distant and vividly real.

Alongside the physical training, mental preparation became just as vital. He dove into strategy books, analyzing plays and drawing inspiration from the football legends he admired. Kurt studied game film, dissecting every successful quarterback, learning from their strategies and mistakes. The grocery store could have been a place of stagnation, but he turned it into a sanctuary for growth, using it as motivation. Every scanned barcode was a reminder of his goals—every customer was a witness to the grand game of his life.

Then, the opportunity to step onto a bigger stage arrived: the Arena Football League. The moment Kurt entered the arena was monumental. With bright lights shining down and an excited crowd buzzing with anticipation, he finally had a chance to showcase his talents. Imagine it—players rushing onto the field, adrenaline pumping, the air crackling with potential. For many, this might have felt like just another day in the minor leagues, but for Kurt, it was a launching pad, an arena of redemption where he could finally let loose.

The games were a whirlwind of excitement. The pace was frenetic, the crowd loud and passionate. It was like football on a caffeine high—an exhilarating mix of speed, strategy, and a dash of chaos. The Arena Football League was unlike anything he'd ever known, where scores could soar in seconds, and the outcome was uncertain until the final whistle blew. It was here that Kurt Warner began to shine, throwing touchdown passes that set off cheers and lifted spirits. Each game was a vibrant reminder of the passion that had fueled his countless nights of hard work and sacrifice.

Playing in the Arena League was more than just about the game; it was a revival of hope. Every touchdown he threw felt like a stamp on his football journey, each one declaring, "I am here, and I am ready." The more he played, the more doors to the NFL started to swing open. He began to catch the eye of scouts and teams. Just imagine the thrill racing through him every time he completed a game-winning touchdown, knowing he was inching closer to the professional league he had dreamed about for so long. The excitement of being back on the field after so much struggle was intoxicating, and every play became a testament to his perseverance.

Throughout this exhilarating journey, Kurt was supported by his family and friends, who cheered him on from the stands. They witnessed the transformation—how a man once weighed down by a grocery store job was now filled with hope and possibility. The camaraderie with his teammates strengthened his resolve; they shared the same dream, a relentless desire to rise above adversity. Every huddle became a meeting of aspirations, and each play drawn on the chalkboard was a step toward making their dreams come true.

Then came the call—the moment that changed everything. The phone rang, slicing through the anticipation and chaos. When Kurt answered, the voice on the other end delivered the news he had been longing to hear: he was invited to join an NFL team. Picture it: his heart raced, disbelief and joy colliding as he absorbed the weight of that moment. His hands trembled, tears welled in his eyes, and he listened as years of hard work transformed into an invitation to greatness. It felt as if the universe had conspired to align his passion and opportunity, finally rewarding him for his unyielding determination against all odds.

Kurt hurried to gather his friends and family to share the momentous news, excitement buzzing through the room like an electric current. They erupted in cheers, laughter, and joyful tears, embracing one another as years of dreaming materialized in that single instant. Imagine the hugs, the high-fives, and the overwhelming wave of relief washing over him as the burdens of the past faded into the background of achievement. All those sleepless nights and grueling workouts morphed into the thrill of possibility—this was the confirmation of a dream that had felt so far away but had always burned brightly within him.

As the adrenaline surged, it wasn't just a call to the NFL; it was a call to a new chapter, a chance to step onto the grand stage he had always longed for. He recognized the weight of this opportunity, a chance to prove himself in a league where legends are made. It wasn't merely about joining a team; it was about making a statement that his journey had led him to this moment of glory, and he was ready to embrace it.

The roar of the crowd awaited him, and for Kurt Warner, every moment leading up to that call had prepared him for this incredible chapter of his life. The years of hard work, the resilience in the face of adversity, and the unwavering commitment to never give up were about to be put to the test on the biggest stage of all. In that moment, with the phone still warm in his hand, he understood that the journey was far from over; it was just beginning.

Belief Beyond Barriers

There's something truly special about the energy in the air just before a football game, especially when it's one of the biggest games of your life. The Super Bowl—an epic battle, the pinnacle of sports—creates an atmosphere buzzing with excitement. For Kurt Warner, this wasn't just another game; it was the result of years spent overcoming challenges and chasing his dreams. Imagine him pacing in the locker room, feeling the tension in the air, while the cheers of fans echoed from outside. In that moment, doubt could creep in, and nerves could get the best of him, but for Warner, this was a chance to unleash the passion and purpose that had guided him through his incredible journey.

Before every game, Kurt had his own set of rituals that transformed the pre-game chaos into a source of strength. He knew the importance of focus, using those last moments in the locker room to connect with himself and his goals. Perhaps he would close his eyes for a moment, visualizing the perfect throws, each spiral landing just right in the hands of his receivers. In his mind, he played out each scenario, anticipating the flow of the game like a conductor leading an orchestra. For him, it was a dance of faith and determination, finely tuned through years of hard work and perseverance.

As the players stepped out of the tunnel, the crowd's roar swelled like a huge wave crashing on the shore. There was something magical about that moment—the bright lights illuminating the field, the jerseys shining, and the heart-pounding rhythm of anticipation. The stadium, a massive arena filled with fans, became a space for transformation. Warner thrived on this energy, channeling it into his deep-seated belief that he belonged on this stage, ready to write a new chapter in his life.

When the opening kickoff soared through the air, all Kurt's past experiences flooded back to him: the moments of doubt, the long nights of practice, and the countless hours spent working in the grocery store, wondering if he would ever get his shot. Each play on the field was a tribute to the struggles he had overcome, showcasing the skills honed through countless scrimmages and the wisdom he gained from studying the game. He wasn't just playing football; he was living a dream that once felt out of reach.

Throughout the game, Kurt showed the leadership and determination that had marked his entire journey. When faced with challenges, he didn't fold under pressure; instead, he thrived. Picture him calling plays with an intensity that could electrify the crowd. As he stood in the huddle, scanning the faces of his teammates, he knew they all shared a common goal. Together, they were united by a vision of victory, driven by the belief that anything was possible if they combined their strength.

Then came the moments that made the game unforgettable. With the score close, every pass he threw was executed flawlessly. Warner's throws sliced through the air like arrows, perfectly spiraled and placed with an artistry developed from years of hard work. The crowd erupted with each touchdown, a sound that resonated deep within him, urging him to push harder. Standing in the end zone after scoring felt like pure bliss—a release of all the years spent striving for this moment.

As the clock ticked down, the weight of the game grew heavier, each second filled with potential and tension. The world outside seemed to disappear; all that existed was the field and the mission at hand. It was as if fate had woven together the threads of his life into this critical instant. With every snap, Kurt felt the energy surge through him, reminding him of his journey, his struggles, and the countless sacrifices made along the way.

With the game on the line, Kurt orchestrated one final drive down the field, summoning every ounce of energy he had left. The feeling was electric; the stakes were sky-high, and with each completed pass, the atmosphere grew thick with excitement. Each time he released the ball, he visualized success, allowing his self-belief to guide his throws. The rhythm of the game mirrored the heartbeat of his dreams—one beat pulsing with hope, the other with a vision slowly becoming reality.

Then it happened—the moment when everything fell into place. The final seconds ticked down, and Kurt stood tall in the pocket, scanning the field like a general ready for battle. He spotted his receiver and let the ball fly. It soared through the air, an elegant arc that felt almost unreal. As the receiver caught it, the cheers erupted into a celebration of joy. In that instant, all doubts and struggles vanished, replaced by the undeniable truth that dreams can come true.

As confetti fell and teammates surrounded him, years of hard work burst forth in a wave of celebration. Kurt Warner had not only won the Super Bowl; he had solidified his legacy as a symbol of hope for dreamers everywhere. His victory was more than just a win on the field—it was a powerful reminder that belief, faith, and determination can help us overcome the challenges life throws our way.

Looking back on his journey, the lessons Warner learned went beyond football; they were about resilience and self-belief. Each obstacle he faced had shaped him, turning him into the player and person he became. The grocery store days faded into the background, just a prelude to the epic story that would inspire generations to come. His journey encouraged countless young athletes to pursue their dreams, reminding them that believing in themselves can ignite the fires of possibility.

As we reflect on Kurt Warner's story, there are many lessons to take away—lessons of hard work, the relentless pursuit of goals, and the unshakeable power of self-belief. Young readers absorbing the essence of his journey are invited to think about their own dreams and ambitions. What challenges might they face? How can they find strength within themselves, just as Kurt did? The answers may not lie in the promise of success, but in the faith that fuels the journey.

Life is filled with ups and downs, twists and turns, but like Warner, anyone can turn challenges into stepping stones. Whether aspiring to be athletes, artists, or leaders in their communities, they can learn from Kurt's example. Every dream starts with a belief, a spark that lights the way, even when the road ahead seems clouded by doubt or fear.

So, as young dreamers hold onto their aspirations, let them carry Kurt's legacy in their hearts. It's a reminder that greatness often comes from struggle, and victory feels sweetest when earned through determination and faith. Let them embrace the journey ahead, trusting in their abilities to break through barriers and achieve the extraordinary, just as Kurt Warner did when he made his mark in football history. The field is waiting, and the dreams are ready to be chased.

W. Bo Cricklewood

Chapter 3: The Unstoppable Jerry Rice: How Hard Work Made a Legend

Humble Beginnings

Jerry Rice didn't just wake up one day to find himself among the football legends. His journey started in a quiet town: Starkville, Mississippi. This is a place where Mississippi State University casts a long shadow, and where everyone knows each other's names. Life here moves at a pace as slow as molasses. It was in this charming Southern town, steeped in family values, that Rice's story took shape, laying the groundwork for the unstoppable force he would later become on the football field.

Born on October 13, 1962, Jerry was the youngest of three siblings. His dad was a hardworking brick mason, and his mom was a devoted schoolteacher. They weren't just parents—they were role models who instilled the values of hard work, determination, and perseverance in their children. The Rice household was full of love, but it also demanded effort. If you wanted something, you didn't just sit around waiting for it to come to you; you had to go out and earn it. This idea was the heartbeat of young Jerry's upbringing.

From a young age, Jerry learned the importance of hard work. His parents stressed education, urging their kids to do well in school while also reminding them that playtime was a chance to build skills. Little Jerry had a special love for sports. Whether he was throwing a football with his siblings in the backyard or running through the fields of their neighborhood, it was clear he was passionate about the game. Yet, as he raced through the grass, feeling the wind at his back, he didn't realize he was laying the groundwork for a future that would take him all the way to the NFL.

In a town like Starkville, Jerry was not just another kid—he stood out. This wasn't only because of his natural athletic talent, but also due to his fierce drive to get better. While other kids were lounging around on weekends, he sought out local high school players. They were bigger, stronger, and had been playing longer, but that didn't scare him; it motivated him. He would watch them, copy their moves, and when he got the chance, he'd jump into their games, soaking up every tip and trick they had to share. This relentless quest for improvement marked the beginning of his journey.

What many didn't see was the tough road that came with his dedication. The local sports scene in Starkville wasn't glamorous. Training facilities, specialized coaching, and top-notch gear were scarce. But what Starkville lacked in resources, it made up for in spirit. Young Jerry often trained in the sweltering heat, using whatever he could find—trees for hurdles, sand for resistance, and the blazing Mississippi sun as his ever-present partner in practice.

Jerry also had a strong support system that pushed him to chase his dreams. His mother often encouraged him to run—not just to build stamina, but to clear his mind. "When you run," she would say, "you get stronger and learn to tackle challenges head-on." That mantra stuck with Jerry throughout his life, becoming more than just advice; it became his way of living.

School wasn't a walk in the park either. While Jerry excelled academically, he had to juggle his schoolwork with demanding practices and games. But he never backed down. He had a clear goal: he wanted to be the best. With each early morning run and every late-night study session, he was carving his path to greatness.

In high school, Jerry's talent truly began to shine. His coach saw his potential and encouraged him to join the varsity team as a sophomore. It was a big leap, but he thrived under the pressure. He quickly established himself as a standout wide receiver, showing off not just his speed but also a knack for making catches look effortless. Teammates and coaches alike started to see that there was something special about this kid from Starkville. He had that spark—the same spark that would eventually fuel a remarkable NFL career.

Despite all his talent, Jerry never got complacent. As he continued to shine, he stayed humble. Every touchdown, every catch was just another step in a long journey. He knew it wasn't just about raw talent; it was about the determination to keep pushing forward, keep improving, and keep dreaming. This foundational belief—valuing effort over entitlement—would become a hallmark of his legendary career.

When Rice transitioned from high school to college football, he did so with the same relentless spirit that had carried him through his youth. He enrolled at Mississippi Valley State University, a school not typically known for churning out NFL stars, but one that offered him the chance to display his skills on a bigger stage. His journey was about to take another exciting turn, but it wouldn't come without challenges.

The college level brought its own set of hurdles. Jerry had to adjust to a new style of play and face opponents who were just as determined as he was. Training became more intense, and the competition tougher. But with each practice, Rice grew more confident in his abilities. He sought out the best players, learned from them, and worked tirelessly to hone his craft.

What really set Jerry apart wasn't just his physical skills but his mental toughness. Every setback turned into a lesson. He learned to keep a positive attitude, even when things didn't go his way. If a game didn't go as planned or he dropped a pass, he wouldn't dwell on it; instead, he would watch the film, analyze what went wrong, and turn it into a learning experience. This ability to bounce back from failure would become a defining feature of his impressive career.

Throughout his college years, Jerry Rice set records and earned accolades that few could match, but he remained that same humble kid from Starkville who took pleasure in the little moments: a perfectly thrown pass, the thrill of scoring a touchdown, and the bonds he shared with his teammates. Little did he know, he was on the brink of greatness—greatness that would inspire countless others. Each record he broke wasn't just a statistic; it was a tribute to his journey—a journey built on the values he learned as a child.

As Jerry got ready to step into the professional world, the lessons from his humble beginnings were always close to his heart. They would drive his work ethic and strengthen his resolve. The challenges he faced were merely stepping stones on his path to becoming one of football's all-time greats. Little did he know, the best was still ahead. And for every young reader and aspiring athlete, there's a lesson in his story: the road to greatness is paved with hard work, humility, and an unshakeable belief in oneself.

Training Like a Champion

The journey to greatness is built on hard work, sweat, and unyielding discipline. When Jerry Rice moved from being a standout college athlete to an NFL superstar, his daily training routine showed that he knew talent alone wouldn't get him to the top. It was his relentless drive to be the best that made him a true champion—a mindset he carried from the fields of Mississippi to the grand stadiums of the NFL.

Picture this: waking up at dawn, when the world is still wrapped in the calm of early morning, with only the soft rustle of leaves and distant bird songs breaking the silence. For Rice, this wasn't just a beautiful scene; it was a sign that training time had arrived. Rising before the sun, he laced up his cleats and prepared for a training session that would challenge him like never before. This morning ritual set the stage for the incredible work ethic that would eventually carve his name into football history.

Each morning kicked off with a tough workout meant to build both strength and stamina. Rice understood how crucial conditioning was, realizing that a well-prepared body could handle the demands of a hard-fought game. He sprinted not just in straight lines, but also through drills that tested his agility and quickness. Imagine him weaving through cones, his feet moving so fast they seemed like a blur, showing that his training wasn't just about speed; it was about being light on his feet and ready to make that game-winning catch.

But speed wasn't everything. Rice included strength training in his routine, lifting weights and doing resistance exercises to build the muscles needed to fend off defenders. His dedication was incredible; he often tackled weights that would intimidate many seasoned athletes. The image of him hoisting heavy bars, sweat glistening on his forehead, became a familiar sight—a true testament to his commitment to outwork anyone in his path.

Rice also understood the importance of perfecting his skills on the field. After his morning workouts, he dedicated hours to running routes, catching passes, and honing his footwork. His hands were his most valuable tools, and he made sure they were as reliable as ever. Whether it was a simple catch or a breathtaking one-handed grab, he practiced them all. Each drill was a repetition that required immense focus, but for Rice, it was all part of the process. In the world of elite athletes, there's no room for anything less than perfect.

Let's not overlook the late-night drills that became a hallmark of Rice's training. While others enjoyed their rest, he was out there under the glow of flickering lights, running routes, catching passes from a quarterback friend, or even tossing the ball against a wall to sharpen his reflexes. It was during these late-night hours that the true champion emerged—the one willing to give up comfort for the sake of greatness. These late-night sessions turned into legends, stories shared in locker rooms and on fields, motivating countless young athletes to find their own training time while the rest of the world was asleep.

One particularly vivid image comes to mind: Rice would often go to a local park where he set up a basketball hoop. He would sprint toward it, leap up to touch the rim, and then sprint back. This wasn't just any exercise; it was a way for him to build explosive strength in his legs—an invaluable asset when leaping for passes. Each jump, each touch of the rim, brought him closer to being the best wide receiver in the game.

Such commitment raises an important question: What are you willing to do to chase your dreams? This challenge echoes throughout the world of sports and beyond. The answer is often found in those late-night drills and early morning workouts. It's in the dedication to do what others won't—a lesson that goes beyond sports and speaks to anyone aiming to reach their fullest potential.

Yet, Rice's training journey wasn't always smooth sailing. Like all athletes, he faced injuries, fatigue, and doubts. During one particularly tough summer, he faced a setback that could have thrown him off course. A minor ankle sprain during practice forced him to take a break. Instead of letting this setback stop him, he turned it into a chance to grow. With a champion's mindset, he focused on improving other areas of his training, such as upper body strength and watching game footage, ensuring that when he returned to the field, he'd come back even stronger.

Rice's attitude showcased his mental toughness. He realized that training was just as much about mental strength as it was about physical strength. Every day brought a new chance to push through discomfort, to silence the fatigue that whispered for him to stop. His mantra became one of resilience—a belief that today's struggles would lead to tomorrow's victories. This mindset created a deep sense of purpose within him; each drop of sweat, each ache in his muscles, was another step toward his dreams.

The impact of Rice's training spread beyond just himself; it inspired teammates and young athletes everywhere. When Rice joined the San Francisco 49ers, his work ethic set a new standard that raised the bar for everyone around him. Teammates admired his dedication, and soon a culture of hard work blossomed in the locker room. Young players looked up to him, eager to learn from his insights and follow in his training footsteps. It wasn't just about one person; it was a movement, a collective push toward greatness.

To illustrate this dynamic further, think of how Rice often invited teammates to join him for morning workouts. The shared experience of running sprints together and cheering each other on created bonds that lasted well beyond the field. It was more than just training; it was proof of teamwork and support, a lesson that would stick with them long after their playing days were over. It showed that when you work hard for something, you're not just chasing personal goals; you're fostering an environment that helps everyone succeed.

As the years rolled on, accolades began to stack up—NFL records, Super Bowl wins, and recognition as one of the greatest players ever. Yet, for Rice, it was never just about the trophies or the spotlight; it was about the journey and the never-ending quest for self-improvement. He often reflected on the countless hours spent training, the sacrifices made, and the lessons learned throughout. Each practice session, each workout, laid a brick in the foundation of his legacy.

This legacy goes beyond broken records and touchdowns; it represents the power of discipline, the value of consistency, and the steadfast commitment to one's goals. Jerry Rice's story serves as a beacon for young athletes, encouraging them to embrace the grind, recognizing that every moment spent training is a step closer to their dreams.

As we move on to the next chapters of Rice's life, keep in mind that greatness rarely happens by chance. It is shaped with purpose, built through hard work, and reinforced by a strong belief in oneself. For every aspiring athlete reading this, consider what it means to train like a champion. It's not just about clocking hours on the field; it's about nurturing a mindset that helps you overcome challenges, pushing you to rise higher and achieve what once seemed impossible. So, ask yourself, are you ready to train like a champion?

Setting Records and Examples
Jerry Rice's football career is an incredible adventure filled with astonishing accomplishments. It's an understatement to say

he merely "set records"; he truly reshaped what it means to be excellent in the sport. When we talk about his impressive career receptions and touchdowns, we're not just rattling off numbers; we're uncovering a story of hard work, determination, and a guide on how to lift not just oneself, but an entire team to new heights.

What stands out most about Rice's achievements isn't just the impressive statistics, though they are certainly remarkable. It's how those figures reflect the values of teamwork and mentorship. Rice didn't just play football; he turned the game into a chance for growth for himself and everyone around him. His astonishing record of 1,549 career receptions isn't just a nod to his talent; it symbolizes his dedication and the strong bonds he built with his teammates. Each time he caught a pass, it represented countless hours of collaboration, trust, and shared dreams.

What makes Rice's journey even more meaningful is how he became a mentor to many players in the locker room. He approached each game with fierce intensity but also recognized the importance of helping others succeed. Young players admired him and often turned to him for advice or just someone to talk to. To them, Rice wasn't just a superstar; he was a guiding light, showing the way with hard work and integrity. His presence both on the field and in the locker room inspired a culture of excellence that reached beyond the game itself.

Imagine being a rookie with the 49ers, walking into a locker room where the legendary Jerry Rice was just a few lockers away. For many, it felt like stepping into a sacred space. They watched his routine, his careful preparation, and how he treated every practice as a chance to sharpen his skills. It wasn't just Rice's physical talent that made an impact; it was the attitude he brought—a constant drive to get better and a deep commitment to the team. He encouraged those around him to take charge of their own journeys, just as he had.

Rice's influence went beyond the field; he filled the locker room with an energy that brought players together. One memorable story from teammates highlights Rice hosting spontaneous training sessions where he invited everyone to join him in drills, no matter their position. He saw the value in each player's role on the team and was eager to help them reach their full potential. With a blend of humor and seriousness, he emphasized the importance of teamwork, which not only improved performance but also created lasting friendships.

One powerful story that showcases Rice's impact is about a rookie receiver who struggled with catching the ball during training camp. Feeling frustrated and defeated, the young player approached Rice for help. Instead of offering just kind words, Rice took the rookie under his wing. He spent hours after practice throwing the ball, sharing tips on how to position his hands, and demonstrating the art of catching. With Rice's patient guidance, the rookie's confidence grew, and he eventually made a vital contribution to the team's success. This transformation perfectly illustrates Rice's legacy—a legacy built on the belief that greatness is never a solo effort.

When we look at Rice's record of 208 career touchdowns, it's easy to focus on the numbers. But this record reveals a lot about his unwavering determination to rise to the occasion time after time. Each touchdown was a moment where Rice not only seized an opportunity but also showcased his instinctive understanding of the game. He had an extraordinary ability to be in the right place at the right moment, turning well-planned plays into unforgettable scoring moments. It wasn't just luck; it was the result of countless hours spent studying plays, analyzing defenses, and honing his skills.

The competitive spirit within Rice pushed him to keep raising the bar. He knew that records weren't just milestones; they were challenges waiting to be met. Every time he stepped onto the field, he had a purpose—not just to score but to inspire others. And inspire he did, through his incredible performances and the way he connected with fans and young athletes. Rice often talked about hard work, perseverance, and believing in oneself, themes that resonated with aspiring players.

Even after retiring, Rice's influence only grew stronger. He became a mentor for young athletes, promoting the values of hard work and resilience. He took on speaking engagements, participated in community events, and led coaching camps to share his knowledge with the next generation. For him, telling his story wasn't about reliving past glories; it was about instilling hope and ambition in those who looked up to him. He encouraged young athletes to aim high and to realize that the path to greatness is often filled with challenges, where each obstacle offers a chance for growth.

Jerry Rice's legacy goes well beyond football; it lives on in the lives he has influenced and the lessons he continues to share. His achievements highlight the power of commitment, the importance of community, and the limitless potential within each of us to inspire and be inspired. While records may be broken, the core values Rice represents— unwavering dedication to excellence and the drive to uplift others—remain timeless.

This lasting spirit is reflected in the stories shared by former teammates and young players who talk about how Rice shaped their lives. Many mention how his example encouraged them to push themselves, embrace the hard work, and recognize that their own success is often tied to the success of those around them. The sense of camaraderie he fostered became a guide for future teams, showing that the journey to greatness is never a solitary one.

Rice's life after football mirrors the same principles he lived by during his playing days. His commitment to mentorship and his tireless effort to motivate others have forged a new role for him as a source of inspiration. He has spoken at countless events, sharing stories from his career to emphasize the lessons he learned along the way. Young athletes listen closely, not just to hear about his many victories, but to grasp the messages of resilience and teamwork that resonate so deeply.

In a world that often shines a light on individual success, Rice's story reminds us that the path to greatness is not one taken alone. As we honor the records he achieved, let's also celebrate the many lives he impacted on his journey. For Jerry Rice, greatness isn't just about touchdowns or receptions; it's about the legacy of mentorship, teamwork, and inspiration that he continues to create. Each young athlete stepping onto a field, driven by Rice's example, carries forward the lessons he shared, ensuring his influence on the sport—and on life—endures for years to come.

Ultimately, Jerry Rice's journey captures the essence of striving for greatness, uplifting others while chasing your dreams, and leaving a lasting mark that goes far beyond the numbers. Whether on the field, in the locker room, or within the community, he embodies the idea that while records may fall, the true impact of what we give to others—our time, our knowledge, and our encouragement—has the power to create a legacy that lasts. The resonance of his achievements continues to inspire young athletes today, reminding them that they, too, can reach for the stars and that their journey can connect with those around them to create a powerful force for good.

Chapter 4: Iron Man: Brett Favre's Incredible Streak of 297 Games

Love for the Game

In the small town of Kiln, Mississippi, where the air feels thick with humidity and the sweet sound of cicadas fills the summer evenings, a young boy named Brett Favre found his passion for football. With a fierce determination that would later shape his legendary career, Brett spent countless hours tossing a football with his friends in their backyards and at local parks. For him, every throw sparked a dream, and every catch brought him one step closer to becoming the quarterback he longed to be.

Brett grew up in a family that cherished sports. His father, Irvin Favre, was a high school football coach, while his mother, Bonita, stood by her husband's love for the game. From the earliest days of his childhood, Brett was surrounded by the spirit of football. But it wasn't just about the sport itself; it was the sense of togetherness, the thrill of competition, and the joy of being part of a team that truly captivated him. Irvin taught Brett not only how to throw a perfect spiral but also the values of hard work, commitment, and respect for the game.

As Brett entered youth leagues, his talent quickly made a name for him. He had a natural gift; his arm could launch the ball deep down the field, and he had the quickness to dodge defenders. But what truly made him stand out was his burning passion. He wasn't playing just to win; he played because the game was a part of who he was. He embraced every opportunity to practice, learn, and improve. Whether he was sweating through drills in the blazing sun or tossing the ball in the backyard under his father's watchful eye, he was driven by a genuine love for football.

Yet, it was more than the excitement of the game that drew Brett in; it was the strong friendships he built with his teammates. The bonds formed on the field created a sense of belonging that extended far beyond the sidelines. They became a close-knit family where victories were shared and losses were met with encouragement. Every huddle, every chat in the locker room, and every post-game talk nurtured friendships that shaped Brett's character and his understanding of teamwork.

As the seasons rolled on, Brett's reputation soared. High school football was the next stage for his growing talent. Playing for Hancock North Central High School, he amazed crowds with his skills. Under the bright lights of Friday night games, he became a warrior; each game was a new battlefield where he showcased not only his athletic abilities but also his leadership. He was more than just a player; he was the quarterback, the one who called the plays and inspired his teammates when challenges loomed.

During this time, whispers of his potential started to spread. Coaches, fellow players, and even fans couldn't help but notice his knack for rising to the occasion. He thrived under pressure. But with all the praise came its share of challenges. He dealt with the common struggles of young athletes: the anxiety of performing, the fear of falling short, and the weight of expectations. Instead of allowing these pressures to overwhelm him, Brett turned them into motivation. He transformed his nerves into fuel, using them to sharpen his skills and prepare for what lay ahead.

One unforgettable moment stands out in his mind—a high-stakes game during his senior year. The opposing team was strong, and the excitement in the air was palpable. Under the buzzing lights of the stadium, Brett felt the energy around him, and he knew this was his time to shine. With the score tied and only seconds left, he gathered his teammates, heart pounding, confidence surging through him.

"Just believe in each other," he urged, his voice steady. "Let's show them what we can do!"

As the last play unfolded, he took the snap, laser-focused. With quick movements, he scanned the field, and despite the pressure, he launched the ball with precision. It soared through the air like a comet, landing perfectly in the hands of his wide receiver, who sprinted into the end zone for the game-winning touchdown. The crowd erupted, but for Brett, this moment was a celebration of his love for football and the teamwork that made it all possible.

This experience lit a fire within Brett—a desire to elevate his game beyond Kiln. As high school ended, he felt the weight of decisions pressing down on him. The opportunity to play at the college level awaited him, but he faced uncertainty about whether he was ready for the challenge.

It was his father who offered clarity. One evening, Irvin sat down with Brett and talked about his dreams. "If you love the game, go after it," he advised. "Don't shy away from hard work or obstacles. They're what make this sport truly rewarding." Those words struck a chord with Brett, pushing him closer to his destiny.

With hope and determination in his heart, Brett decided to play for the University of Southern Mississippi. There, he faced new challenges, including the demands of college life and competition from other talented players. Yet, his love for football only grew stronger. Every practice was a chance to learn and improve, and every game was an opportunity to showcase the skills he had developed over the years.

What truly distinguished Brett from others was his determination to face adversity head-on. When faced with criticism or setbacks, he pressed on with resilience. He realized that achieving greatness was no easy feat. It demanded sacrifice, grit, and an unwavering love for the game that flowed through him. The bonds he formed with his teammates helped him navigate the tough times. They supported each other, creating a brotherhood that extended beyond the field.

As his college journey progressed, so did his dreams of playing in the NFL. Each game became a stepping stone toward that coveted goal. Coaches noticed his skills and leadership, while scouts began to take interest. Even as the spotlight brightened, Brett remained humble, always remembering where his passion began.

In the end, it was that same love for football, deeply rooted in his heart, that propelled him into a historic career. His journey would lead him to heights he had only dared to dream of, resulting in a remarkable streak that would engrave his name in football history. With every snap and every throw, he carried the spirit of that young boy from Mississippi—the boy who discovered endless possibilities through football.

The love for the game is a powerful force, one that can change lives, inspire greatness, and build unbreakable friendships. Brett Favre's story began in Kiln, but it was just the start of an epic journey filled with triumph, determination, and an unshakeable belief in the magic of football. The lessons learned and the friendships formed along the way would leave a lasting impact on many lives, including his own.

In the world of football, where dreams are chased and legacies created, the heart of a true athlete beats strongest when driven by a relentless love for the game. This is a story that speaks to young athletes everywhere, reminding them that passion and hard work can lead them to greatness, both on the field and in life.

Facing Adversity Head-On

Brett Favre's story is not just about talent and victories; it's a vivid journey marked by hardship and perseverance. The path to the NFL, and his incredible streak of 297 consecutive games played, was filled with hurdles that tested his physical strength and mental resilience. From injuries that threatened to keep him off the field to personal losses that shook him deeply, Favre confronted these challenges with a determination that would define his legendary career.

In the demanding world of professional football, injuries happen all the time, and Favre was no stranger to their harsh realities. His body bore the scars of a sport that can be unforgiving. But what set him apart was not just his ability to play through pain, but his relentless drive to step onto the field week after week, no matter the obstacles he faced. One game stands out in everyone's memory: the time Favre played with a cracked rib.

Picture this: a freezing winter night, the atmosphere thick with excitement. Favre, the unyielding warrior, stands tall in the pocket, fully aware that he's not at his best. The pain coursed through him, but in that moment, it was overwhelmed by something stronger—his commitment to his teammates and fans. He knew that the jersey he wore was more than just clothing; it symbolized loyalty, dedication, and pride. "I owe it to them," he thought. This conviction pushed him to take the snap, evade defenders, and make throws that highlighted his incredible skill despite his injury.

After the game, Favre shared that the pain was worth it, as he hoped to inspire his teammates. His commitment became a rallying cry for the entire team. They didn't see him just as a quarterback; they viewed him as a leader willing to brave tough conditions, beat the odds, and endure discomfort to keep their dreams alive. To Favre, every injury was just another chapter in his ongoing saga, a testament to the grit that would shape his legacy.

But the injuries were only part of his story. Off the field, Favre faced a personal tragedy that changed everything. The sudden loss of his father, Irvin, was a life-altering blow. Irvin wasn't just a father; he was a coach, a mentor, and a guiding light for Brett. Their bond was built on a shared love for football and countless lessons learned on the sidelines. When Irvin passed away, Brett was left carrying a weight that felt nearly unbearable.

Yet, true to Favre's spirit, he turned that heartbreak into a way to honor his father's memory. Just hours after the loss, he stepped onto the field to face the Oakland Raiders, his heart heavy but his determination unshaken. He played with a passion that went beyond the game; it was a performance driven by emotion and a desire to pay tribute to a man who had taught him the values of hard work and resilience. "My dad would've wanted me to play," he later reflected. And play he did, throwing for four touchdowns and leading the Green Bay Packers to a significant win.

That game was a crucial moment not only in Favre's career but in his life. The support he received from fans, teammates, and even rivals reinforced the idea that football is more than just a game; it's a community that comes together during tough times. Favre's ability to transform his personal pain into powerful performances resonated with fans everywhere, solidifying his place as a sports icon. His story of resilience became part of football's greater narrative, showing how the sport can heal and unite.

Even amid these tough experiences, Favre maintained a light-hearted spirit that endeared him to fans. His playful antics, often shared through funny stories, remind us that even the toughest competitors can have a fun side. Imagine him pulling pranks on teammates or cracking jokes in the huddle—these moments of laughter were essential, balancing the seriousness of his struggles with joy that brightened the locker room. Favre had a special gift for making the game enjoyable, reminding everyone that competing is important, but so is having fun along the way.

The mix of his serious side and his ability to lift spirits shows us that being resilient doesn't mean lacking joy. It's about finding happiness in the midst of challenges. As Favre dealt with injuries, loss, and the pressures of fame, he found comfort in laughter and camaraderie with those around him. This blend of strength and humor made him relatable, especially to young fans who looked up to him.

Brett's journey teaches us an important lesson: facing challenges is part of being human. It's not the setbacks that define us, but how we respond to them. Through pain and loss, Favre didn't just emerge as a remarkable player; he became a symbol of resilience, proving that we can confront life's storms with courage and grace.

Looking back on these challenges, it's clear that Favre's story is one of growth and change. Each injury became a chance to show his toughness. Each loss was an opportunity to come back stronger, not just for himself but for those around him. He learned that being vulnerable can be a source of strength, and that sharing our struggles can connect us and inspire others.

As fans continue to celebrate his incredible streak and legacy, they should remember the spirit that drove him. Favre's journey reminds us that adversity is not an ending; it can be a stepping stone to greatness. Whether it's stepping onto the field with cracked ribs or channeling personal grief into an extraordinary game, Brett Favre's legacy highlights the human spirit's ability to face challenges directly.

In a world where difficulties are unavoidable, Favre's story serves as a source of encouragement for young athletes, urging them to embrace their struggles, learn from their experiences, and stay determined in their goals. Through every twist and turn in his career, Favre demonstrated that true strength lies in persistence, finding joy in the journey, and inspiring those around us. The laughter, heartaches, and victories of Brett Favre paint a picture of an athlete who was not just playing a game but living a life rich with lessons on resilience and an unshakeable love for football.

Indeed, it's an inspiring legacy that continues to motivate young athletes to tap into their inner strength and tackle their own challenges, one snap at a time. As we explore the depths of his journey, we discover not just a player, but a person who embraced the game with passion, faced his trials with unwavering determination, and became a beacon of hope for anyone chasing their dreams. Brett Favre's story reminds us that while the game can be tough, so are the ones who dare to play it.

The Meaning of Resilience

Brett Favre's incredible journey in the world of football serves as a powerful reminder that true success isn't just about awards or records. It's rooted in our ability to rise, adapt, and thrive in the face of challenges. When we think about Favre's legacy, it's clear that his story is much more than just the games he played or the touchdowns he scored. It embodies a spirit that inspires countless individuals, especially young athletes, to face their own hurdles with courage.

Favre's story is packed with lessons that anyone who's faced setbacks can relate to. From the very first time he put on a football jersey, it was obvious he had a remarkable passion for the game. But it was how he handled the obstacles that came his way—whether it was injuries or tough losses—that made him a true legend. His journey shows us that resilience isn't just a single event; it's a lifelong process filled with struggles, challenges, and victories.

Think about Favre's remarkable streak of 297 consecutive games played. While many celebrate this record, each game comes with its own story of determination. The pain he endured, the doubts he faced, and the moments of vulnerability that turned into strength are all part of what made him who he is. Favre's love for football shone through, even as he dealt with injuries that could have stopped many players in their tracks. This teaches us that the game is more than just physical skill; it's about heart, mind, and the unyielding spirit to rise again after life knocks us down.

This brings us to what resilience really is: the choice to respond positively to challenges. Favre's life encourages us to take a moment for some self-reflection. What challenges are you facing right now? Are you struggling with fears of failure in sports or school, or perhaps dealing with personal issues that feel overwhelming? Recognizing these challenges is the first step toward building your own resilience. Just like Favre, we must learn to embrace discomfort, knowing that it can lead to growth.

Let's not forget Favre's famous quote: "The only thing I ever wanted to do was play football." This simple statement captures his dedication and love for the game, but it also suggests a deeper lesson about life. It's about finding what you're passionate about and holding onto it, no matter what obstacles come your way. As young readers, it's important to understand that passions can grow and develop, even when faced with difficulties. Just like Favre, who played through painful injuries and personal losses, you too can learn to keep going.

Encouraging readers to write down their thoughts about personal challenges can be a great way to build resilience. When they jot down their struggles and set goals to overcome them, they're creating a roadmap for their journey. This isn't just about writing down hardships; it's about picturing success and figuring out the steps to get there. With every word in their Score Journal, young athletes can turn their experiences into action plans, much like Favre did on the field.

As Favre faced various challenges, he didn't just survive; he thrived. His story shows us that resilience isn't about never facing setbacks; it's about how we bounce back from them. When injuries knocked him out of the game, he didn't see them as defeats; he viewed them as chances to come back stronger and wiser. In life, every challenge can be seen as a stepping stone rather than a stumbling block. This mindset is vital for young athletes aiming to be champions, both on the field and in life.

Furthermore, Favre's story highlights how important community is when it comes to building resilience. He didn't go through his journey alone; his teammates, coaches, and fans were crucial to his success. The support he received became a source of strength. Young readers should be encouraged to create their own support networks—whether through family, friends, or teammates. By sharing struggles and victories, we learn that resilience is often strengthened through the encouragement of others.

In addition to his physical skills and leadership on the field, Favre was known for his vibrant personality. He brought joy and laughter to a game that could be very serious, reminding us that resilience can coexist with joy. Those light moments amidst fierce competition show that humor can help us cope with the pressures we face. Favre's playful spirit is a reminder to not take life too seriously and to find happiness even in challenging situations.

As we celebrate Brett Favre's legacy, we recognize the power of passion, perseverance, and the human spirit. His life is filled with inspiring quotes that reflect what football—and life—mean to him. "I just want to be the best I can be," he often said, showcasing a commitment to continuous growth. This is a message young athletes should keep in mind: strive for personal excellence and embrace the journey, no matter the ups and downs.

So, as young readers navigate their own paths, let them draw inspiration from Favre's extraordinary journey. Every player, every student, and every dreamer has the potential to create their own remarkable story. By embodying the spirit of resilience, they can learn to confront their fears, face challenges, and bounce back from setbacks. Each of these experiences, just like Favre's, adds a meaningful chapter to their lives, filled with lessons learned and strength gained.

In short, Brett Favre's journey teaches us that resilience isn't just about getting back up; it's about the attitude we bring to our challenges. It's about finding meaning in our struggles and allowing that meaning to drive our passion. Through his story, young athletes are invited to see that every challenge is a chance to grow, adapt, and thrive, just as Favre did.

As they lace up their cleats and step onto the field, they should remember they carry within them the same spirit that propelled Brett Favre to greatness. The road may be tough, but like Favre, they have the potential to become champions—not just in sports, but in life. It's a journey worth pursuing, and they hold the power to turn their dreams into reality, one play at a time.

W. Bo Cricklewood

Chapter 5: The Sweetness of Success: Walter Payton's Amazing Story

Early Challenges and Big Dreams

Columbia, Mississippi, in the late 1950s wasn't exactly an easy place for a young boy to grow up, especially if that boy was Walter Payton. This small community, with its friendly neighborhoods where everyone knew each other, often smelled of delicious Southern cooking. But underneath that cozy surface, life could be tough. Payton's family, like many others in the area, struggled to make ends meet. His father worked at a factory, and his mother took care of the home and kids.

They worked hard to support their three children and taught Walter and his siblings the values of dedication and perseverance.

From a young age, Walter Payton showed an incredible talent for sports, especially football. Columbia didn't have fancy facilities or tons of resources, but Walter found joy in playing on muddy fields and makeshift pitches around the town. It was during these casual games that he began to develop his amazing skills—running, dodging, and outsmarting his opponents. Each time he touched the ball, he felt a spark ignite inside him—a dream of achieving greatness that would take him to heights few could ever imagine.

However, dreaming big in Columbia came with its challenges. Payton faced societal issues that could easily crush the spirit of any young athlete. Racial barriers loomed large in the world of sports, often leading people to underestimate the abilities of talented African American players. In this atmosphere of doubt, skepticism became a constant companion for Payton, who fought against the low expectations placed on him. Yet, this very doubt became the fuel that ignited his determination, sparking a fire within him that couldn't be put out.

A turning point in his young life arrived when Walter played his first organized football game. It was a sunny autumn afternoon, and excitement filled the air as young athletes prepared to showcase their talents. Wearing an oversized jersey and shorts, Payton was more than just nervous—he was eager. As he stepped onto the field, he felt the weight of not just his dreams but also the hopes of his family on his shoulders. His heart raced as he lined up against the opposing team, but the thrill of the competition soon replaced his nerves.

From the very first whistle, Payton's raw talent shone bright. He ran like a whirlwind, weaving through defenders with a grace that seemed almost magical, his feet barely touching the ground. The cheers from his teammates and the gasps of the crowd blended into a powerful wave of support that pushed him even harder. With each successful play, he experienced the joy of victory. But it wasn't just about winning; it was about the pure love of playing the game he cherished.

After that first game, it was clear that Payton's talent had not gone unnoticed. His coaches recognized his potential and encouraged him to work even harder, helping him develop his skills further. The respect he earned on the field became the foundation for his growing career, but it was the support he received at home that truly kept him grounded. His parents, despite their own struggles, never missed a chance to cheer Walter on. They provided him with love and the belief that he could achieve greatness, no matter what challenges came his way.

Family support can be a guiding light in uncertain times, and for Walter, it was no different. His mother often reminded him, "Walter, always believe in yourself, even if others don't." Those words echoed in his mind whenever he faced the challenges that came with being a gifted athlete in a world full of doubt. When other kids teased him, claiming he would never play for a college team, Walter only grew more determined.

By the time he reached high school, the whispers of his talent had turned into a roar. Payton broke records week after week, running with a speed and agility that left defenders in the dust. Each game was not just a performance; it was a declaration. He wasn't just another player; he was Walter Payton, and he had arrived. College scouts began to take notice, and with that attention came the realization that his dreams were within reach.

Yet, even as he dazzled on the field, the skepticism never fully faded away. Questions about whether he could truly succeed at the next level hung in the air, creating a constant reminder of doubt. But rather than let those doubts hold him back, Walter used them as motivation. With every setback and negative comment, he pushed himself harder, determined to prove everyone wrong.

The legendary high school career that followed showcased his resilience and spirit. His performance was so electrifying that it looked like he was dancing with the football, effortlessly weaving in and out of defenders in a way that captivated everyone watching. Week after week, he set new records, creating benchmarks for future athletes to strive for.

And while Payton's feet carried him across the field, his heart was always in Columbia. He often returned to his neighborhood to inspire younger kids, showing them that their dreams were within reach. Walter didn't just want to be a star; he wanted to uplift those around him, demonstrating that with hard work and dedication, anything was possible.

As his high school career came to a close, new opportunities blossomed. Walter received scholarship offers from various colleges, each one a promise to help him grow into the athlete he aspired to be. But he knew these offers were not just for him; they symbolized hope for others in his community. Each acceptance letter was a step toward proving that hard work and determination could conquer any challenge.

These early obstacles shaped Walter Payton into a person who would be remembered not just for his skills on the football field but for his character and heart off of it. He became a figure of inspiration for many, a shining example that while dreams may start in humble places, they can reach incredible heights. Walter Payton's story is one of grit, determination, and an unshakeable belief in oneself—a narrative that resonates not only in the world of sports but in the hearts of anyone who dares to dream.

Reflecting back, Walter would realize that the struggles of his youth weren't setbacks but stepping stones, preparing him for the success that lay ahead. His journey had only just begun, but the lessons learned during those formative years would lay the groundwork for a legacy that would last a lifetime.

Teamwork and Talent

Walter Payton's time at Jackson State University was a key part of his life. It wasn't just about honing his skills on the football field; it was about the friendships he built and the lessons he learned about how teamwork can make all the difference. During these years, he developed a strong work ethic, a sense of camaraderie, and an incredible talent that not only elevated his game but also inspired everyone around him.

Training sessions were tough, often starting before the sun rose. With the first light barely shining, Payton would lace up his cleats, ready to tackle the day. His commitment was clear. While many saw long days filled with drills as a chore, Walter saw them as a chance to improve. He often stayed after practice to run extra sprints, fine-tune his footwork, and push himself in ways that left his teammates amazed.

"Why do you put in all this extra work?" a teammate once asked, breathless after a tough workout. Walter just smiled and answered, "Because I know I can be better. And if I can be better, then we can be better." It wasn't just about his own improvement; it was about lifting everyone up, creating a culture of success that echoed throughout the team. His dedication inspired his teammates to step up their game too.

Teamwork flourished at Jackson State. Walter wasn't just a player; he was a leader who recognized the value of helping others as he climbed the ladder of success. The friendships made in those locker rooms and on the field weren't just casual connections; they were built on mutual respect, shared challenges, and a common dream of greatness. They experienced the highs and lows together, realizing that a strong team could face any obstacle, both on and off the field.

One unforgettable moment happened during a particularly tough game against a rival school. The atmosphere was charged, filled with passionate fans and the intense energy of competition. Payton's team was trailing, and morale was low. The players looked to their captain, but instead of giving in to despair, he rallied them. "Hey! We're not done yet!" he shouted, his voice breaking through the fog of doubt. "We have each other, and that's enough!" His enthusiasm reignited the team's spirit, leading to an incredible comeback that ended in a thrilling victory.

Walter's talent for motivating his teammates became legendary. He had a unique gift for sensing when someone was struggling and knowing just what to say to lift their spirits. "You can do this!" he would shout from the sidelines when he saw a teammate falter. "You're a beast! Show them what you've got!" His words were contagious. With each shout of encouragement, players felt like they could take on the world.

The importance of teamwork went beyond the field. Walter took part in community outreach programs, showing his teammates that their efforts could reach far beyond football. Whether he was organizing charity events or visiting schools to inspire young athletes, Payton's commitment to giving back helped create a sense of unity and purpose within the team. He understood that success isn't just about personal accomplishments, but about making a positive impact in the lives of others.

As he moved into the NFL, these values stayed with Walter. The Chicago Bears embraced him, and he quickly became an essential part of the team. His athletic ability allowed him to make jaw-dropping plays, darting through defenses like a gazelle. But it was his leadership and capacity to inspire that turned the Bears into a powerful force. His teammates looked to him not just for guidance but for hope, and he was always there to lend his support.

One particularly touching story from his early NFL days involved a rookie running back who had just been drafted. The young player arrived with huge expectations and nerves that could shake a wall. In the locker room before his first game, the tension was palpable. Walter took a moment to sit beside him, offering wise advice that would stick with the young player long after the game ended. "Just breathe. Remember why you love this game. You're not alone out there. We're a team, and we've got each other's backs."

That rookie went on to have a great debut, but it was Walter's calming presence that made a lasting impression. He knew that teamwork was about more than just physical skill. It was about building connections, trust, and lifting each other up amid the chaos that often comes with being on the field. This was a lesson he learned in college and carried into his professional career.

Of course, there were tough times too. Like any athlete, Payton faced challenges and setbacks, but it was in these moments that he truly shined. He often said that tough times show what people are made of, and he was committed to showing resilience when things got rough. When the team faced a series of losses, he reminded his teammates that it wasn't the end. "Every champion was once a contender that refused to give up," he would say, his unwavering spirit shining like a beacon during stormy times.

Outside of football, Walter's philanthropic work grew. His efforts to uplift the community reflected the values he developed at Jackson State. The same determination he put into football was now focused on making a difference in the world. He organized charity events, engaged with young players, and created opportunities for others to succeed, proving that while individual talent is impressive, it's the collective effort that truly makes an impact.

Every encounter he had with aspiring athletes reminded him that everyone has their own journey. By sharing his story and emphasizing the value of teamwork, he inspired countless kids to dream big and work hard. One young athlete, a boy from a tough neighborhood, listened in awe as Walter spoke about his own beginnings and the importance of perseverance. The boy later shared, "He made me believe that if I work hard enough, I could get there too. If he can do it, why can't I?"

This sense of hope—of lifting each other up to reach for the stars—deeply resonated with Payton. It wasn't just about his own success, but about encouraging those around him to pursue their greatness. He understood that success is much sweeter when it's shared and that every victory is a testament to the support and hard work of the whole team.

As he continued his career, Walter always remembered the lessons he learned at

Jackson State University. Those experiences shaped him into a player who was as much a team player as he was a superstar. He kept proving that while individual talent is amazing, it's the strength of a united team that can turn dreams into reality. The friendships made and spirits lifted would always be part of who he was.

Walter Payton's story is one of grit, determination, and a strong belief in the power of teamwork. It serves as a reminder to young readers that they're not alone in their journeys and that together, they can tackle any challenge. True success comes not only from personal achievements but from the connections we create and the support we offer each other. In this beautiful dance of talent and teamwork, we find the true spirit of achievement.

Giving Back and the Legacy of Sweetness

Walter Payton was more than just an amazing football player; he was a true friend to many, someone whose kindness and generosity went far beyond the field. While his record-breaking runs and dazzling plays captured the hearts of millions, it was his deep commitment to helping others that really showed why he was called "Sweetness." In a time when many athletes get lost in fame, Payton consistently chose to use his spotlight to do good, proving that real compassion can ring louder than any crowd's cheer for a touchdown.

In 1999, he founded the Walter Payton Foundation, which became a key way for him to give back to the community he cherished. This foundation focused on helping children and families who were facing tough times. Walter's passion for this cause stemmed from his own experiences growing up and understanding what hardship felt like. Coming from humble beginnings, he knew that having support could change someone's life. The foundation's programs included scholarships for underprivileged kids, food drives, and holiday gift-giving events. Each effort was a testament to his belief that everyone deserves a shot at success, no matter their situation.

One touching story that highlights Payton's work involves a young boy named Marcus. Born with a serious illness, Marcus spent much of his childhood in and out of hospitals. He often felt lonely, longing for friends and hope. When the Walter Payton Foundation learned about him, Walter took the time to visit Marcus in the hospital. With a warm smile and a gentle spirit, he spent hours playing games and sharing stories about his life in football. By the time he left, Marcus felt something he hadn't experienced in a long time—a flicker of hope.

"Mr. Payton showed me that I could still dream big," Marcus later said. "He made me feel like I mattered, even when things were tough." This kind of connection wasn't just a one-time event; it was a reflection of how Payton lived his life, always seeking ways to uplift others and bring joy to their days. Stories like this were common through the foundation's work, each one a powerful reminder of how one person's kindness can leave a lasting mark on many lives.

Payton's caring spirit extended to various causes he truly believed in. He was especially devoted to children's health and education. He often visited local schools, sharing stories of perseverance, teamwork, and hard work with students. These visits weren't just about football; they were about inspiring young minds to pursue their dreams. Payton encouraged kids to believe in themselves and stressed the importance of education, showing them that success isn't just about being the best athlete.

During one school assembly, Payton shared an important lesson with a group of eager children: "You don't have to be the best at everything to succeed. What matters is that you try your hardest and never give up. Even if you fall down, you get back up and keep moving forward!" His words struck a chord, motivating many kids to put more effort into their studies and sports. The laughter and excitement in the room showed just how impactful he truly was.

Additionally, Payton was a strong advocate for health issues, especially those affecting young people. His own battles with health problems later in life pushed him to raise awareness about conditions that could be improved with better lifestyle choices. He participated in campaigns promoting heart health, making it clear that taking care of oneself is just as crucial as striving for greatness in sports. His message was simple: a healthy body supports a healthy mind, allowing people to chase their passions with energy.

Among his many initiatives, one that really stood out was a community football clinic he hosted each summer. Young athletes from all backgrounds eagerly came to learn from the legendary player. But what Payton offered went beyond football skills; he instilled the values of hard work, teamwork, and a sense of community. "Football is about teamwork," he would remind them. "It's not just about the plays you make; it's about lifting each other up."

Parents often watched in amazement as Walter engaged with their kids, treating each one like family. His warmth and sincerity made every participant feel valued. One parent remarked, "Walter didn't just teach my son how to run faster or throw better. He taught him how to be a good person." Payton's influence spread far and wide, creating a legacy that went well beyond the game of football.

Looking back at Walter Payton's life, it's clear that his legacy of kindness and giving still inspires not just those who were lucky enough to know him but also a new generation of athletes who look up to him. Many current players see Payton as a guiding light, encouraging them to give back to their communities and use their fame for positive change. Stars like Drew Brees and Russell Wilson often express how Payton's example motivated them to get involved and make a difference. It serves as a powerful reminder that true greatness isn't just about winning games; it's about the positive impact you have on others.

While Payton's legacy lives on through countless charitable efforts and inspiring stories, the most meaningful part of his legacy is probably the message of love, humility, and giving back. It invites all of us to reflect on how we can contribute to our communities and think about the ways we can make a difference, no matter how big or small.

As we work to create a kinder world, let's remember that even the smallest acts of kindness can create waves of change. The stories of those whose lives were touched by

Walter Payton stand as a powerful reminder of this idea. They show us that behind every achievement, there's an opportunity to lift others, spread joy, and nurture hope.

Ultimately, Walter Payton's impact reaches far beyond his amazing touchdowns or record-breaking seasons. It's found in the hearts he touched and the lives he changed. His lasting legacy encourages all of us to be better, show kindness, and strive for greatness—not just for ourselves, but for those around us. Every little act of kindness adds to a bigger story of hope and connection. Walter Payton taught us that being a champion isn't only about collecting trophies; it's about how we use our time and talents to uplift others, creating a sweet legacy that can endure for generations.

W. Bo Cricklewood

Chapter 6: The Miracle Catch: David Tyree's Super Bowl Moment

An Unexpected Hero

In a world where sports often seem dominated by towering giants and flashy talent, David Tyree's story stands out as a beacon of perseverance and self-belief. Imagine a young boy, much like many of you, dreaming of catching the winning touchdown in a crucial game. But for David, those dreams were often clouded by doubts and challenges that felt overwhelming. He didn't come from a family of athletes, nor was he the most naturally gifted player on the field. Instead, David was the underdog—a shining example that heroes don't always show up with trophies and accolades.

Growing up in a lively city, David's childhood wasn't the kind of privileged experience you might associate with a future NFL star. Raised in a neighborhood rich with stories and filled with laughter and competition, he discovered his passion for football on the playgrounds nearby. Yet, while others seemed to fly past him, David often struggled, battling insecurities that would test anyone's spirit. "Imagine being told you're not good enough over and over again," he once shared. "That's a tough pill to swallow, but I choked it down and kept pushing forward."

High school was a tough time for David, a real battleground where he faced the constant whispers of doubt that threatened to overwhelm him. His teammates were tall, fast, and already attracting attention from college scouts. Meanwhile, David was often overlooked, playing in the shadow of those destined for greatness. He faced fierce competition, wrestling not just against other athletes but against his own fear of failing. It would have been easy for him to give up, to walk away from sports altogether, but that wasn't David's approach.

Rather than give in to the naysayers, he turned that negativity into motivation. Each drop of sweat on the practice field was a sign of his commitment to his dreams. He became a player determined to define himself, not by others' opinions, but by his own hard work. The practice field became a sanctuary for him, a place where he could unleash his full potential. It was here he learned a crucial lesson: hard work triumphs when talent doesn't put in the effort.

David's college journey at Syracuse University marked a significant turning point in his life, a proving ground where he finally began to shine. Picture being on a team filled with players eyeing the NFL, knowing you have to fight for your spot. David felt this pressure deeply. With sheer grit and determination, he began to carve out his legacy. "Every single day was an opportunity to prove them wrong," he said, capturing the essence of a true fighter.

As he sharpened his skills, it became evident that David had something unique: an unstoppable tenacity. In practice, he was tireless, determined to not only catch the ball but to seize every opportunity that came his way. It was during this time he realized that stars aren't just born; they are forged through hard work and resilience.

David's hard work did not go unnoticed. After college, he was chosen in the sixth round of the 2003 NFL Draft by the New York Giants. While some might see a sixth-round pick as an afterthought, for David, it was a chance—a golden opportunity to step onto the biggest stage in sports. When that call came in, it felt as though all those years of sweat, tears, and determination had led to that one triumphant moment. "I was just happy to be part of something bigger than myself," he reflected.

What truly made David Tyree an unexpected hero was not just his journey to the NFL, but how he carried the lessons from his past into his future. He embodied resilience, reminding us that the journey often holds more significance than the destination. Each setback, each moment of doubt, became a stepping stone toward greatness.

Thinking about David's story, we see a powerful reminder that while the spotlight often shines on the brightest stars, it is the journey—the struggles and triumphs—that shape who we become. David Tyree's path from the sidelines to the Super Bowl shows that sometimes, the most remarkable heroes emerge from the most humble beginnings. With grit, determination, and an unwavering belief in oneself, anyone can beat the odds and craft their own incredible story.

The Catch That Shocked the World

Imagine this: Super Bowl XLII is unfolding in all its glory, and millions around the world are glued to their screens. The atmosphere is charged with excitement as the New York Giants prepare to challenge the undefeated New England Patriots. With just minutes left in the game, everything hangs in the balance. Fans are on the edge of their seats, hearts racing as they sense they are witnessing something that could change the course of sports history forever.

The scoreboard shows a tight 14-10 in favor of the Patriots, and the Giants face an uphill battle. They're not just playing for the trophy; they're aiming to carve their name into NFL history by defeating a team that has dominated the season without a loss. Eli Manning, their courageous quarterback, understands that this moment requires not just talent but an unshakeable faith in their ability to overcome the odds. All eyes are on them, everyone holding their breath, waiting for something incredible to happen.

In the huddle, the air buzzes with a mix of urgency and hope. Eli looks around at his teammates, and they all feel the weight of the moment. "We can do this," he says, his voice steady and full of passion. It's like a spark of confidence igniting in the middle of a storm. The players nod, drawing strength from their leader, ready to rise to the challenge and perhaps create a bit of history along the way.

As the play gets underway, fans can hardly keep their excitement in check. The clock ticks down, and with each passing second, the suspense grows. The tension is thick as the Giants face a Patriots defense that has been relentless all season. The crowd is a mixture of gasps and cheers, a single heartbeat of hope and anxiety, as Eli takes the snap.

In those critical moments, the defense closes in, but Eli remains calm. With sheer determination, he scans the field for an opportunity. The Giants have fought through challenges all year, and now they need to draw on every lesson learned and ounce of grit they've built. Fans are glued to the action, as if time has slowed, the noise of the crowd fading into a low hum.

David Tyree, who has often found himself in the background throughout his career, knows this is his time to shine. He positions himself just right, and with each stride, he feels the weight of his journey pushing him forward. This isn't just another play; it's the result of years of hard work and determination. His heart races, fueled not by fear, but by a thrilling mix of adrenaline and purpose.

As Eli releases the ball, the world seems to hold its breath. Time stretches as the football spirals through the air, heading straight for David, who is closely guarded by the Patriots' defense. The crowd collectively pauses, captivated by the unfolding drama.

Here it comes—the moment that could make or break a dream.

In an instant, David leaps into the air, but that's not the end of the story. As he jumps, a defender collides with him, and in that split second, he instinctively pins the ball against his helmet. It's a move that seems impossible, defying both logic and gravity. The football sticks to his helmet as if by magic. The crowd erupts, transforming from anxious silence into a roaring explosion of disbelief. "Did that really just happen?" one fan yells, while another breaks into an ecstatic cheer.

This wasn't just a catch; it was a powerful statement, showing that sometimes the impossible can come to life. In that fleeting moment, David Tyree became a symbol of hope for every underdog out there. The famous helmet catch, now etched in NFL history, stands as a tribute to resilience and the strength of will. Giants fans spring from their seats, their cheers reverberating throughout the stadium. The energy of the moment resonates far beyond the game, inspiring countless dreamers who believe in the impossible.

But the excitement doesn't stop there. Eli and David's connection ignites a spark that propels the Giants forward. They charge down the field, each play filled with renewed belief and fierce determination to claim the championship that once felt out of reach. The crowd is electric, chanting and cheering, pouring their energy into every moment.

With every yard gained, the Giants aren't just moving the ball; they're rewriting history. Fans are fully absorbed in the experience, united in their thrill as they watch the dramatic events unfold. The stadium erupts with each successful play, bringing them ever closer to a potential victory.

As the clock ticks down, excitement builds to a fever pitch. It's a moment bursting with possibilities, where dreams feel within reach. The Giants cross the goal line for the winning touchdown, and the explosion of joy that follows is beyond anything the stadium has ever witnessed.

David's catch wasn't just a showcase of athleticism; it lit a fire of hope. That single moment shifted the game, proving that greatness can come from the most surprising places. With the Giants clinching their victory over the previously unbeaten Patriots, a new chapter in sports history is written. David Tyree's name will forever be remembered by fans, becoming a symbol of triumph over challenges, reminding us that the heart of sports lies not just in winning, but in the stories that encourage us to pursue our dreams.

Amid the celebratory chaos, with confetti flying and the Lombardi Trophy shining bright, the significance of that moment becomes clear. David Tyree stands as a beacon of perseverance, showing that sometimes the most extraordinary heroes come from the shadows, ready to seize their moment when it counts the most. The Giants' win over the Patriots is a powerful reminder that, in life just like in sports, the impossible can turn into reality with grit, determination, and a steadfast belief in oneself.

Prepared for Greatness

Greatness doesn't just fall into your lap like a lucky surprise from above. Instead, it's something you build over time through hard work, dedication, and a strong commitment to your goals. Take David Tyree's famous catch during Super Bowl XLII, for example. That wasn't just luck; it was the result of years of preparation, both on the field and behind the scenes. When you look closely, you see a powerful story about the importance of hard work and the relentless chase for excellence.

David's journey started long before that unforgettable moment in the Super Bowl. Every practice session, every weight he lifted, and every drop of sweat he shed in training helped him grab that once-in-a-lifetime opportunity. He trained like a skilled artisan refining his craft, pushing himself to become something remarkable. As someone once said about David's path to success, "He had been preparing for this his entire life. Every practice, every workout, every moment spent sharpening his skills was leading him to this game."

This level of dedication didn't just come from a wish to be good. It was fueled by a deep-seated belief that every little bit of effort adds up to something significant. Athletes like David know that the real magic is found not only in those brief moments of victory but also in the countless hours of unseen work that come before. It's this hidden grind that sets champions apart from those who only dream of being champions.

Let's think about the weight room for a moment. It's a place where athletes like Tyree build both their physical and mental strength. The sounds of weights clanging, feet thudding on treadmills, and the focused intensity of their determination aren't just background noise; they're the soundtrack of preparation. For David, every drop of sweat during those tough workouts was a step toward his ultimate goal. Every time he pushed through the pain, he was not just training his body but also toughening his mind for the challenges ahead.

But being prepared isn't just about physical training. It also includes mental and emotional readiness. It's about gearing yourself up to handle not only success but also failure. The road to greatness is often filled with bumps, and being able to deal with those bumps with resilience is what truly prepares someone for success. By the time David reached that game, he had already faced his share of setbacks throughout his career. Each disappointment only made him stronger, teaching him that failure isn't the end—it's a lesson, a necessary part of the journey to greatness.

Young athletes often dream about talent, but while talent is important, it's preparation that transforms that potential into actual performance. This is a vital lesson to grasp. What steps are you taking to get ready for your own moment of greatness? Are you practicing hard enough? Are you working on both your physical and mental skills? David's story is more than just a tale of athletic skill; it's a call to young athletes everywhere. The truth is that every great athlete has faced struggles and sacrifices, and every journey has a starting point.

Take a moment to think about the sacrifices that come with chasing greatness. It often means missing social gatherings, skipping late nights out with friends, and spending weekends training instead of unwinding. It can feel isolating at times, as life continues around you while you're focused on your goals. Yet, every hour you spend improving your craft lays a strong foundation for your future. This level of commitment might seem intimidating, but those who choose to embrace it set themselves apart.

A well-known coach once said, "Success is where preparation and opportunity meet." So when the spotlight is on, and everyone is watching, will you be ready? David's helmet catch is the perfect example of this idea. He didn't just get lucky; he had been preparing, both mentally and physically, long before that ball was thrown his way.

To drive this point home, think about the many athletes who have achieved greatness through sheer determination. Icons like Michael Jordan, Serena Williams, and Tom Brady didn't just spring into success; their stories are filled with hard work and relentless effort. They encountered challenges, setbacks, and doubters along the way, but they never gave up. They dedicated their time and energy to preparation, making sure they were ready to grab their moment when it arrived.

By adopting a mindset of continuous improvement, young athletes can turn their dreams into reality. It's not just about going through the same drills repeatedly; it's about realizing that every practice brings you closer to mastery. It's about spotting weaknesses and facing them head-on. Whether that means fine-tuning your technique, building your endurance, or studying game footage, every effort counts.

Sports have a unique ability to teach lessons that go beyond the field. The lessons of preparation, resilience, and grit apply to all aspects of life. Think about it: how often do we find ourselves facing an opportunity, only to discover we weren't quite ready to take advantage of it? The same preparation that leads to success in sports can pave the way for achievements in school, work, and personal relationships.

As you reflect on your own path, consider the times when opportunity knocked. Were you ready? Did you have the skills and the mindset to seize that moment? Take inspiration from David Tyree's journey; embrace the struggle, refine your craft, and understand that greatness is formed through hard work and preparation. As you move forward, let this question linger in your mind: How are you preparing for your own moment of greatness?

Every day offers a chance to inch closer to your goals. Even when the path seems long and filled with challenges, your hard work can lead to amazing results. David's journey didn't happen overnight; it was built piece by piece, day by day. For every moment of celebration on the field, there were countless hours of dedication behind the scenes.

So what does being prepared really mean? It means taking charge of your future, diving fully into your training, and continually pushing yourself to achieve more. It's about nurturing a mindset of growth, recognizing that there's always room to improve, and understanding that every experience—good or bad—is a stepping stone on your journey.

As you think about your own journey, remember that greatness isn't just for a select few; it's within reach for anyone who is willing to put in the effort. Every person has the potential to rise above the ordinary and create their own success story. It all begins with a commitment—to practice, to learn, to grow.

Ultimately, David Tyree's famous catch is a powerful reminder of the incredible potential that exists within all of us. The magic of that moment wasn't just in the act itself; it was all the hard work that led up to it. The sacrifices, the sweat, and the unyielding quest for excellence set the stage for his greatness. So go ahead and challenge yourself. Embrace the journey. Because, as David showed us, your moment of greatness might just be waiting for you to grab it with both hands.

W. Bo Cricklewood

Chapter 7: The Comeback King: Joe Montana and The Drive

Cool Under Pressure

In the world of football, where tension simmers like a pot ready to boil over, one man truly stood out for his coolness under pressure. Joe Montana, a name that echoes through NFL history, earned his reputation not just from his incredible talent but by staying calm in the most intense moments. Picture yourself in a massive stadium, where thousands of eyes are glued to you, the air buzzing with excitement, and the fate of the game resting on your shoulders. This was Montana's stage, and he thrived under pressure like a sunflower reaching for the sun.

Joe's journey started in the small town of Monongahela, Pennsylvania, where every kid dreamed big. With a football in hand, he wasn't just another face in the crowd; he was a force to be reckoned with. While other kids might have buckled under the first sign of trouble, Joe seemed to welcome it. It was as if he found joy in overcoming challenges, shaping a mindset that would support him through the most critical moments of his career.

What made Montana stand out from many of his peers was his incredible ability to stay calm as the clock wound down. Think of it like being on a rollercoaster. As you climb that steep hill, your heart races, your palms sweat, and your mind buzzes with excitement and fear. But just when you think it can't get any more intense, the drop hits, and instead of screaming, you throw your hands in the air and enjoy the ride. That was Montana on the football field. He wasn't just another player; he was the one steering the experience with grace.

In college at Notre Dame, Joe learned early how to handle the pressure that came with being in the spotlight. One of the most memorable moments was during the 1977 Sugar Bowl against the University of Alabama. The Fighting Irish were down, and Montana was surrounded by doubt and criticism. But instead of letting the pressure crush him, he turned it into fuel. With precision, he executed one play after another, ultimately leading his team to an unbelievable comeback victory. The excitement of that win was contagious, and it firmly established Montana's reputation as someone who could shine when the stakes were highest.

As he entered the NFL, those skills he developed in college only grew stronger. In a game where wins and losses can hinge on mere seconds, staying focused and calm becomes crucial. The San Francisco 49ers quickly discovered that they had not only drafted a talented quarterback but also found a leader who would guide them through tough times. Imagine a packed stadium, fans roaring like lions, opposing players fierce and determined, and all eyes fixed on one man. For most, that scene would trigger anxiety. But not for Joe.

During his time with the 49ers, Montana faced some of the most intense situations imaginable. In 1982, during a playoff game against the Dallas Cowboys, the 49ers were trailing in the final moments. The atmosphere was thick with tension, and it seemed like all hope was fading. Yet, Montana stood firm. Instead of panicking, he called the plays with a calm confidence that made his teammates trust him. He famously rallied his team with a sense of assurance that said, "We can do this." As the clock ticked down, Montana delivered a perfect pass to Dwight Clark, who made the iconic catch that sent the 49ers to the Super Bowl. This moment, often called "The Catch," captured Montana's incredible knack for not just handling pressure but rising above it.

Mental toughness played a key role in Joe's success. Imagine sitting in a math class, staring at an impossible exam. Many students might buckle under the weight of expectations, but the truly resilient ones take a deep breath, focus, and break the problem into smaller pieces. Montana approached each game similarly. He had a unique mental game that helped him visualize success, tune out distractions, and stay focused on what mattered. Before every snap, he took a moment to breathe, center himself, and remind himself of all those hours of practice that brought him to that very moment.

One of the hallmarks of Montana's playing style was his ability to remain unflustered, even when chaos erupted around him. Picture a chef in a busy restaurant, pots boiling over, orders flying in, and customers growing impatient. While a novice chef might panic, the seasoned professional thrives, orchestrating a symphony of flavors and dishes. That was Joe Montana. He not only stayed calm but also directed the action around him with such effortless grace that it seemed simple.

Throughout his amazing career, he often found himself in high-pressure situations that would send chills down the spine of even the toughest athletes. Yet, where others might see obstacles, Montana spotted opportunities. He frequently shared how he thrived on the adrenaline of the game, using it as energy to drive him forward. This mindset didn't just shine through during games but also in practices, where he encouraged his teammates to push their limits and discover their own strengths.

It's important to see that Montana's calmness wasn't just a natural gift; it was a skill he developed. For young athletes, this is a key takeaway. It's one thing to have talent; it's another to use that talent when facing challenges. Joe was a pro at managing expectations—his own and those of the fans, coaches, and players around him. By viewing pressure as a part of the game, he turned potential disasters into moments of triumph.

Leadership was also a big part of Montana's legacy. While he could throw a touchdown pass like no one else, it was his ability to inspire those around him that truly set him apart. Teammates turned to him not just for his skills but for his unwavering confidence during tough times. They trusted him, not because he was perfect, but because he had an incredible knack for bringing them together when it mattered. This is a valuable lesson for young readers: it's not enough to be the best; you also need to lift others up and create a sense of unity within your team.

In a world where sports can sometimes get lost in drama and controversy, Joe Montana stands out as a shining example of how staying calm and focusing on what truly matters can lead to amazing success. He showed that keeping your cool is a superpower, especially when the pressure is on. It's about being present, believing in yourself, and having the courage to face challenges head-on. For aspiring athletes and dreamers, this message resonates far beyond the football field.

As we reflect on Joe Montana's legendary career, the stories of his remarkable calmness under pressure remind us that greatness isn't just about stats or championships; it's about how one responds when it really counts. In a world full of distractions and noise, being able to stay composed can change the game. This quality not only defines a great athlete but also shapes leaders in every area of life.

The message is clear: when faced with challenges, find your center, take a deep breath, and trust in the training and preparation that led you to this moment. Joe Montana did just that, making him not only an incredible athlete but also a lasting symbol of resilience and calmness under pressure. As we continue to explore his career, it's clear that his story is not just about winning games but about the journey of maintaining composure in the storm—a lesson that speaks to all of us, both on and off the field.

The Legendary Drive

Super Bowl XXIII, held on January 22, 1989, is remembered not just for the teams on the field but for one unforgettable moment—what many now call "The Drive." This incredible series of plays not only shaped

Joe Montana's legacy as a quarterback but also highlighted his strong leadership and the tight bond within the San Francisco 49ers. With the Cincinnati Bengals standing in their way, the pressure was thick, and the stakes couldn't have been higher.

Picture the scene: a packed stadium, fans buzzing with anticipation, each person perched on the edge of their seat. The 49ers were trailing by three points with just over three minutes left on the clock. For many players, this would be a nerve-wracking situation, but for Montana, it was just another day at the office. He thrived under pressure, turning tension into purpose.

The 49ers took the field starting at their own eight-yard line, a spot that would have discouraged most teams. But Joe Montana—calm, composed, and ready—gathered his teammates in the huddle. He viewed the game not merely as a series of plays but as a shared experience built on trust, teamwork, and strategy. His teammates could sense his confidence; it lit a spark of hope in a challenging moment.

Montana kicked off the drive with a simple pass to running back Roger Craig. While it was a cautious beginning, it set the tone for what was to come. This wasn't just about moving the ball; it was about establishing a rhythm and reassuring his teammates that they could tackle the obstacles ahead. Craig, with his sure hands and quick feet, managed to dart up the field for a modest gain of eight yards, and just like that, the 49ers were off to a good start.

Then came a key moment—Montana executed a clever play-action pass to wide receiver John Taylor, who sprinted down the field, evading defenders like a dancer gliding through a crowd. This smart strategy made it seem as if the 49ers were going for a run, pulling defenders closer to the line. The defense fell for it, giving Montana the critical seconds he needed to make the throw. The ball sailed through the air, hitting Taylor in stride. This play earned them another first down, and with each successful move, their momentum grew.

Montana's leadership shined bright in these moments—not just through his actions but through his words. He encouraged his teammates, reminding them of their strengths and capabilities. Each pass became more than just a play; it was a sign of trust—trust that Montana had in his teammates and that they had in him. They all knew that every inch gained brought them one step closer to victory.

As the drive progressed, they encountered a significant hurdle. The Bengals' defense, fierce and determined, tightened their grip, creating pressure on Montana. Time was slipping away, and doubts began to creep in. Yet, instead of letting anxiety take hold, the 49ers rose to the occasion, pushing back against the shadows of uncertainty. Montana, ever the strategist, guided the next phase of the drive, calling for a series of short passes to exploit the Bengals' defensive strategy.

One of those passes went to tight end Brent Jones, who, with surprising agility, maneuvered through defenders for another first down. Montana's ability to read the game and adjust his plays was remarkable. He understood that it wasn't just about sticking to a game plan; it was about adapting and responding in real-time—something only the best athletes can do.

With just a minute left and the 49ers now within striking distance, Montana sensed victory. He made a beautiful throw to John Taylor, who was waiting in the end zone. The atmosphere was electric, and you could feel the excitement in the air. When the ball left Montana's hand, time seemed to slow, and all eyes were glued to the spiraling pass, its fate hanging in the balance like a tightrope walker inching across a high wire.

When Taylor caught the ball for the game-winning touchdown, the stadium erupted into a wild celebration. The cheers rang out like a joyous anthem that filled the air. But for Montana, this wasn't just a win for himself; it was a celebration of teamwork, trust, and collaboration. "The Drive" was not just his triumph; it was a victory they all shared, a powerful reminder of how unity can conquer adversity.

The importance of that drive goes beyond just the final score. It reveals a core truth about sports: while individual talent can shine, it's the teamwork and connection among players that truly elevate a team. Montana understood that every pass, every block, and every catch required harmony and understanding. The 49ers didn't just win; they strengthened their bond, coming together even more resilient than before.

"The Drive" encapsulates a remarkable moment not just in Montana's career but also in the world of sports. It shows that perseverance, smart execution, and strong belief can change the outcome of a game. The camaraderie built in those critical moments, the silent understanding among teammates, and their faith in one another's abilities all played a part in this unforgettable victory.

Reflecting on this legendary drive, we can see it mirrors life itself. Every challenge can seem overwhelming, with obstacles stacked high. Yet, just like Montana, we can find strength in our preparation, trust in our teammates, and the determination to keep moving forward, inching closer to our own goals. The thrill of that game-winning moment and the roar of the crowd remind us that great achievements often come from working together, adapting, and believing in ourselves and each other.

Ultimately, Montana's "Drive" during Super Bowl XXIII is more than just a spectacular moment in sports; it offers a lasting lesson in teamwork, strategy, and the profound strength that arises when we support one another. It inspires us to recognize that when we pool our talents and push ahead together, even the most daunting challenges can turn into amazing victories.

Leadership Lessons

In the constantly changing world of sports, the remarkable people who rise to the top often share a wealth of insights about leadership, resilience, and motivation. Joe Montana, a name that shines brightly in the history of football, didn't just shine on the field; he was a true leader during key moments in games and in everyday interactions with his teammates. His journey offers a wonderful opportunity for young readers to discover important leadership lessons—lessons that apply not only in sports but also in school, friendships, and life as a whole.

Often, leadership is thought of as being the loudest voice, the person who pushes the team to win. However, Montana's approach was different; his leadership was subtle yet incredibly impactful. He showed us that real leaders are not just those who shout orders. Instead, they inspire others through their actions and attitudes, demonstrating commitment, integrity, and a willingness to stand side by side with their teammates.

Think about how Montana took on the role of a leader. He often led by example, showing an incredible work ethic during practices. He wasn't just there to call the plays; he actively participated, putting in the effort day after day. His hard work motivated his teammates. They watched him practice tirelessly, throwing countless passes to improve his skills. Each drop of sweat reflected his dedication to the game and to his team, and that passion was contagious. Young readers might wonder: how do you show your commitment in your own activities? Whether it's working hard for a sports team, preparing for an important test, or collaborating on a group project, consistent effort can inspire those around you.

Another key part of Montana's success was his ability to communicate well. Leadership isn't only about having skills; it's also about building connections. He was approachable, the kind of quarterback who listened as much as he spoke. The huddle wasn't just a place to strategize; it was a space for discussion, encouragement, and support. When he spoke, his teammates felt heard and appreciated, their ideas valued even in the high-pressure moments of a game. The 49ers relied on him not just for his talent but for his ability to bring everyone together and lift spirits.

Young readers can think about how they can be more approachable in their own lives. Do they create an atmosphere where friends feel comfortable sharing their ideas and worries? Whether in sports, school clubs, or daily conversations, being a good listener can change the dynamics of a group, building trust and teamwork.

Now, let's talk about the often-ignored quality of keeping a positive attitude, especially when faced with tough situations. Montana was famous for his resilience, particularly in high-pressure moments. He had a special ability to stay calm when everything seemed to be falling apart. Picture being in a close game, the clock winding down, and the outcome uncertain. Amidst the chaos, Montana focused with a clarity that was almost unbelievable. He didn't just deal with pressure; he thrived on it.

This ability to stay positive in the face of challenges is a lesson that resonates with everyone, especially young readers. Life is full of difficulties, whether it's tackling a tough subject in school, dealing with complicated friendships, or aiming to reach a personal goal. The key is to develop an inner calm and to trust in one's ability to overcome hurdles. It's about looking for solutions rather than dwelling on problems.

A great example of this is a moment from Montana's career when it felt like everything was stacked against him. In the 1982 NFC Championship Game against the Dallas Cowboys, a legendary matchup that defined both Montana and his team, they were down by a touchdown with just seconds left on the clock. Instead of giving in to despair, Montana radiated confidence, leading his team with smart plays that ended in a thrilling victory. His spirit of optimism was infectious, rallying his teammates to believe in the unbelievable, even when it seemed impossible.

As young readers reflect on their own experiences, they can think about times when they've faced challenges. How did they react? Did they let the pressure get to them, or did they channel that energy into finding a solution? Encouraging them to think about these moments can help them see their own potential for leadership, especially during tough times.

It's also important to remember that leadership isn't just about personal qualities; it's about inspiring and uplifting others. Montana had a gift for spotting his teammates' strengths and using them when it mattered most. He understood that a good leader surrounds themselves with capable people and creates an environment where everyone can shine. This is an important lesson for young readers: leadership is not a solo journey; it's about helping others grow alongside you.

To nurture a sense of shared success, readers can think about times they've helped a friend or teammate do well. Maybe they offered encouragement before a big game, assisted with a challenging project, or simply provided support when someone needed it. These acts are not just kindness; they are real examples of leadership in action.

As we reflect on Montana's legacy, let's encourage young readers to consider their own leadership potential. What special strengths do they have that could inspire those around them? Perhaps they excel in creativity, organization, or teamwork. Helping them identify their qualities can motivate them to take on leadership roles, whether at school or among their friends.

Here's something for readers to think about: recall a moment when you stepped up as a leader, even in a small way. Maybe you organized a game during recess, helped plan a school event, or took the lead in a group project. Write down what pushed you to take that step and how it felt to support others.

Reflecting on these experiences can help young readers see themselves as potential leaders, ready to tackle life's challenges.

In the end, the lessons we learn from Joe Montana's leadership go far beyond the world of football; they can be applied to many areas of life. The world needs leaders—people who act with integrity, communicate openly, and maintain a positive attitude. Whether in the classroom, on the playground, or at home, there are countless opportunities to inspire and uplift those around us.

As we move forward, let's keep these lessons in mind. Joe Montana's story highlights the powerful impact of effective leadership, reminding us that every moment offers a chance to inspire others, to create a positive atmosphere, and to embrace the qualities that define true leaders. So the next time you encounter a challenge, remember what leadership really means, as embodied by Montana: it's about leading by example, supporting your teammates, and staying steady when things get tough. Each of us has the potential to be a leader in our own way, ready to make a difference in our communities and beyond.

W. Bo Cricklewood

Chapter 8: Beast Mode: Marshawn Lynch's Unstoppable Spirit

The Power of Passion

When you think of Marshawn Lynch, you might picture a force of nature—fierce, explosive, and truly unstoppable. The football field became his stage, where he delivered performances that could rival the best Broadway shows. His running style was more than just crossing the goal line; it was like a poetic dance of strength and elegance, a thrilling display of his love for the game. Every time he took the snap, you could feel the excitement in the stadium grow, because fans knew they were about to witness something remarkable.

The 2011 playoffs are forever etched in football history, especially one unforgettable moment—the legendary "Beast Quake." Imagine this: the New Orleans Saints were up against the Seattle Seahawks in a first-round playoff game. The atmosphere was electric, and the stakes couldn't have been higher. Marshawn Lynch, donning his iconic "beast mode" persona, took the handoff and launched into a run that would send ripples through the sports world.

As he sped past defenders, Lynch wasn't just dodging tackles; he was powering through them. One Saint after another tried to stop him, but like a tidal wave, he brushed them aside, refusing to let anything stand in his way. The raw intensity of his running left both fans and opponents breathless. It was a moment that perfectly captured his passion for football. With each powerful stride, he represented the spirit of competition, determination, and a love for the game that couldn't be contained. The crowd erupted in a mix of disbelief and joy as Lynch crossed into the end zone, cementing his place in football history.

What truly sets Lynch apart is not just his athleticism but the heart behind his game. "I just love to play the game," he shared, and those words resonate deeply with anyone who has ever felt the thrill of their favorite sport. For Lynch, football wasn't just a job or a way to gain fame; it was a passion that radiated from him, a joy that flowed through every play. This love was contagious, attracting teammates, fans, and even those who might not have been into football.

In an interview, Lynch further opened up about his relationship with the sport. "You gotta take care of what you love," he said, showing that his passion was serious business. It wasn't a casual hobby; it was a commitment that called for hard work and sacrifice. This powerful idea is something young athletes can really connect with. It encourages them to dive into their passions fully, putting their hearts into whatever they love—whether it's football, art, music, or anything else that sparks their excitement.

As we look at Lynch's legacy, it's clear that passion was his secret weapon. It fueled moments of brilliance on the field, transforming games into epic tales of victory. Each time he laced up his cleats, he brought a contagious energy that inspired his teammates and thrilled the fans. His electrifying runs, filled with determination, taught young athletes a valuable lesson: when you chase what you love with genuine enthusiasm, you can achieve incredible things.

Marshawn Lynch's story reminds us that every athlete has their unique style and rhythm. While some players may shine through finesse and agility, others, like Lynch, find their strength in raw power and grit. What truly mattered was that he played to his strengths and stayed authentic. This sincerity is what made him a cherished figure in the sports world.

It's crucial to remember that tapping into passion isn't always easy. There will be moments of doubt, injury, and setbacks that challenge even the most dedicated athletes. Yet, Lynch's journey shows that with perseverance, fueled by passion, you can overcome obstacles. The challenges he faced only made him stronger, paving a path of hard work and determination.

When young athletes watch Lynch's stunning plays, they're not just seeing great athleticism; they're absorbing a powerful lesson. They understand that love for the game can break down barriers, and that passion can light the way to greatness. Whether it's having the confidence to make the winning play or the bravery to push through pain, Lynch's legacy inspires young people to discover their unique voices and let them shine.

This authenticity, this commitment to being true to oneself, is what makes Marshawn Lynch more than just a player; he's a phenomenon. He embodies the idea that being yourself isn't just okay; it's something to celebrate. Lynch's lively personality and his readiness to stand out encourage young athletes to embrace their individuality. His genuine love for the game motivates them to boldly follow their passions, carve out their paths, and write their own stories.

As young readers soak in Lynch's thrilling runs, it's vital for them to see that each play is a celebration of his passion. Every touchdown, every leap, every moment spent on that field was about so much more than just numbers. It was about the joy of playing, the excitement of competition, and the fire in his heart that made it all worthwhile. For those who aspire to greatness, Lynch's journey serves as a guiding light, reminding them that it's possible to channel passion into amazing achievements.

Marshawn Lynch's story is not just about football; it's a rallying cry for anyone who dares to follow their heart. His life teaches us that when you play with passion, you can turn the ordinary into the extraordinary. Whether on the field or off, that unstoppable spirit is a lesson that every young athlete can take to heart. They, too, can find their own "Beast Mode," tapping into their inner drive and showing it to the world. The power of passion is a force that can lift them to heights they might never have imagined, echoing Lynch's legacy in their hearts as they chase their dreams.

Embracing Uniqueness

Marshawn Lynch stands tall as a shining example of being true to oneself in a world that often pushes people to conform. His journey in the world of football isn't just a story filled with touchdowns and tackles; it's a brilliant showcase of self-expression and authenticity. For Lynch, the football field was more than just a place to compete; it was a canvas where he could reveal his unique identity. In a sport where many athletes feel the need to fit into set roles, Lynch broke the mold and showed how beautiful it is to embrace who you really are.

One of the most recognizable parts of Lynch's persona is his iconic "Beast Mode." This phrase has become tied to his fierce playing style and larger-than-life character. But it's more than just a catchy slogan; it captures Lynch's whole approach to both football and life. He stormed onto the field with a bold attitude that screamed, "I'm here, and I'm not going anywhere." His runs weren't just about gaining yards; they were about making a statement. Watching Lynch in full "Beast Mode" wasn't just about witnessing athletic skill; it was an experience that celebrated individuality.

Outside of football, Lynch's interactions with the media revealed even more about who he is. Instead of avoiding the spotlight, he embraced it on his own terms. With a playful and often cheeky spirit, he transformed press conferences into his own show. Who could forget his memorable line, "I'm just here so I won't get fined"? In that simple statement, he captured not only his unwillingness to conform to the typical athlete stereotype but also his determination to play by his own rules. Lynch demonstrated that being yourself can be just as powerful as any touchdown.

The joy he brought to these moments added another layer to his public image. Lynch's humor and charm drew in fans from all walks of life, sending a message that it's okay to be different — in fact, it should be celebrated! His lighthearted approach became a beacon for those who felt like outsiders, resonating with anyone who has ever felt pressure to fit in. In each playful exchange, he reminded us that embracing who we are can create genuine connections, both on and off the field.

Lynch's commitment to advocating for mental health and social justice gives even more depth to his individuality. He understands that being a professional athlete is a privilege, but it also comes with responsibilities. In a society that often brushes mental health under the rug, Lynch openly discusses these issues. He shines a light on the challenges athletes face, challenging the idea that they must always show strength and invincibility. By sharing his experiences, he encourages others to seek help and support, proving that showing vulnerability is not a weakness but a part of being human.

His advocacy goes beyond just talking; it shows in his actions. Lynch actively participates in community outreach, using his voice to uplift important causes that often go unnoticed. His philanthropic work is rooted in a genuine desire to make a difference, especially for those who may not have the same opportunities. By standing up for meaningful issues, he sets an example of how individuality can spark collective change. More than just an impressive player, he is a source of hope for many navigating their own unique paths.

A standout moment showcasing Lynch's unique character happened during Super Bowl media day when he wore a fluffy hat that looked like an animal's head. It was a bold statement, a conversation starter that proved his commitment to standing out. Instead of following the usual paths that many athletes take, Lynch chose to wear his most distinctive accessory, letting his personality shine through. He knows that life is too short to play it safe, and every quirky trait contributes to who he is.

Fans of Lynch see a part of themselves in his refusal to conform to societal expectations. The joy he brings to the field is contagious, spilling over into the lives of those who cheer for him. When he breaks through the defensive line, it isn't just a gain for the Seahawks; it feels like a win for anyone brave enough to be different. His success serves as a reminder that embracing one's uniqueness can lead to incredible achievements. It reinforces the idea that individuality isn't just a characteristic; it can be a superpower.

The bond Lynch has built with his fans is truly special. He has fostered a community that celebrates individuality and self-acceptance. Fans from various backgrounds find common ground in Lynch's playful spirit and fierce determination. Whether they're wearing a "Beast Mode" shirt or rocking a Lynch-inspired hairstyle, they proudly show their admiration. In this way, he has become more than just a football player; he is a cultural icon who inspires others to embrace their quirks and celebrate their differences.

It's crucial to understand that embracing uniqueness doesn't always come easy. The world can be tough for those who choose to defy the norm. Lynch has faced criticism for his unconventional ways and has often been misunderstood. However, rather than letting negativity bring him down, he uses it as motivation to express himself even more. This is a powerful lesson for all of us: when faced with challenges, the strength of your character can shine even brighter.

In times of uncertainty, Lynch's journey offers guidance for young athletes and individuals everywhere. It encourages them to tap into their confidence and authenticity. Celebrating who you are doesn't just lead to self-acceptance; it opens up new opportunities and connections that might have otherwise remained closed. By following Lynch's example, anyone can learn to channel their inner strength and find a place where they truly feel at home.

At its core, the story of Marshawn Lynch is one of celebration, authenticity, and the fearless pursuit of being yourself. As fans reflect on his unforgettable plays, lighthearted moments, and heartfelt advocacy, they are reminded that true greatness comes from being unapologetically you. Lynch's journey is a rallying call for all who aspire to greatness: embrace who you are, flaws and all. Let your uniqueness lead the way, and you might just create a legacy that resonates far beyond the football field.

Playing for the Love of the Game

Marshawn Lynch is more than just a football player; he's a shining example of how joy and passion are at the heart of the game. From the first time he donned his helmet to the electrifying moments of being cheered on by the crowd, Lynch's bond with football was more than just about winning. It was a lively connection, a joyful engagement with a sport he loved deeply. Every time he touched the ball, it wasn't just about scoring points; it was about celebrating the game itself.

Imagine the scene: a packed stadium filled with fans, the smell of popcorn in the air, and chants of his name ringing out. Lynch bursts onto the field, a whirlwind of energy with a smile that could brighten the darkest night. With his unique style and infectious excitement, he approached each play with a childlike joy that drew people in. Watching him play was like seeing a man who knew football was a gift—something he cherished with all his heart.

His celebrations were unforgettable—spinning footballs, choreographed dances, and loud high-fives with teammates were all part of the Marshawn Lynch experience. These moments didn't just capture the joy of scoring; they reminded everyone that success isn't just about stats or trophies. It's about enjoying the journey and the friendships made along the way. Lynch understood this perfectly, and he lived it every time he stepped onto the field.

But Lynch's playful spirit didn't stop at football. He was deeply committed to his community, believing in the importance of giving back. His love for the game extended far beyond the end zone, especially in his hometown of Oakland, California. He dedicated himself to uplifting those around him, particularly children, by investing time and resources in the next generation. His annual football camps, which attract eager kids from all over, are a testament to his belief that sports can change lives.

At these camps, Lynch doesn't just coach; he becomes a mentor. He shares stories from his own journey and emphasizes that success is about more than just winning games—it's about finding joy in what you do. The kids listen intently, soaking in not only football tips but also important life lessons. "Have fun out there," he often tells them, a simple yet powerful message that captures the spirit of why he plays. For Lynch, striving for excellence should always come with the joy of the experience.

Through various outreach programs, he has raised money to support youth sports, advocating for every child to have access to play, no matter their background. He knows that for many young athletes, the chance to participate can be a lifeline, a way to turn their energy and dreams into something real. Lynch has said, "If I can inspire just one kid to pick up a ball and play, then I've done my job." That simple idea is the foundation of everything he does.

Lynch's influence reaches far beyond football fields and charity events. He connects with kids through his fun social media presence, sharing humorous videos, taking part in challenges, or just engaging with fans. This interaction isn't just about building a brand; it's about creating a sense of community and showing young people that being themselves is the best way to be.

Even off the field, Lynch's love for the game shines through in how he interacts with fans. He takes the time to chat with young supporters, posing for pictures and sharing laughs. In these moments, he isn't just a famous NFL player; he's a friend, a role model, and a source of inspiration. The joy he brings to their faces highlights the idea that sports are meant to be enjoyed together, forging connections that last long after the game ends.

Think of the countless times Lynch has made headlines—not just for his athletic skills, but for the warmth and joy he brings to every encounter. During a memorable visit to a local hospital, he surprised children facing tough battles by wearing a custom "Beast Mode" cape, bringing laughter and positivity to a place often filled with challenges. His cheerful spirit brightened the room, reminding everyone that happiness can be found even in difficult times.

Lynch's genuine love for football and his community stands out in a world that often judges success only by trophies and accolades. For him, the journey has always mattered more than the end result. He has shown repeatedly that life isn't just about winning; it's about making moments that matter, sharing experiences, and building relationships.

The message he shares is clear: play for the love of the game. This isn't just a catchy phrase; it's a way of life that encourages everyone—especially young athletes—to dive into their passions with excitement. When you play for the love of the game, you tap into an experience that goes beyond competition. You become part of something bigger, a community that celebrates your uniqueness, your victories, and the lessons learned along the way.

In a world full of pressure to be perfect, Lynch shines as a guiding light, showing the way to being true to oneself. He demonstrates that the real measure of success is found in laughter shared with teammates, the sweat on your jersey, and the buzzing energy of the crowd cheering you on. His story inspires young athletes to fully embrace their passions and remember that, above all else, sports are meant to be fun.

To understand Marshawn Lynch is to grasp the true essence of football—a beautiful game full of heart, spirit, and community. The sweet moments of victory are enhanced by the friendships formed, the challenges faced, and the sheer enjoyment that comes with every snap of the ball. He urges kids to discover their joy in the sport, whether on a grand field or in their own backyard, reminding them that passion fuels greatness.

So as young athletes tie their cleats and get ready for their next game, let them carry Lynch's spirit with them. Let them soak in every tackle, every touchdown celebration, and every laugh shared with friends. Because in doing so, they're not just playing a game; they're creating memories, building connections, and most importantly, finding joy in what they love. It's this powerful message—the importance of finding happiness in every moment—that Lynch has shared with countless lives, reminding us all that success is about the joy we create, not just the trophies we win.

Marshawn Lynch leaves a legacy that goes beyond the football field. He teaches us that the heart of any endeavor lies in its ability to spread joy—not just to the players, but to everyone involved. So as we think about his incredible journey, let's remember to celebrate the game, the friendships, and the joy it brings to our lives. Just like Lynch does, let's always play for the love of the game.

Chapter 9: The Immaculate Reception: Franco Harris Makes History

A Play for the Ages

The energy at Three Rivers Stadium on that chilly December afternoon in 1972 was electric, buzzing with the hopes and dreams of Pittsburgh Steelers fans packed into the stands, dressed in black and gold, ready to witness a showdown that would become legendary. As the clock ticked down toward what could have been a crushing defeat or a chance for glory, the excitement was so thick you could almost touch it. It was the AFC Wild Card game, a do-or-die situation that could define not just the season for the Steelers, but possibly shape the future of the franchise.

On the sidelines, Franco Harris stood amidst the whirlwind, his gaze fixed on the unfolding drama. The young running back, a rookie drafted in the first round earlier that year, had already faced more than his share of challenges. The whispers of doubt that followed him into the league had faded into a distant memory, replaced by the steady beat of his own heart, a reminder of the weight of the moment. He was ready, even if he wasn't the star of the play designed by head coach Chuck Noll.

As quarterback Terry Bradshaw dropped back, the crowd collectively held its breath, a wave of hope and anxiety crashing against the shores of expectation. There was a rhythm to it all—each heartbeat syncing with the dwindling seconds of the game. Bradshaw scanned the field, his eyes darting like a hawk searching for its next meal, until they locked onto John "Frenchy" Fuqua, the intended receiver. Bradshaw launched the ball, its spiral slicing through the air like a comet on a collision course.

Then, in a split second, everything changed. Fuqua collided with Raiders safety Jack Tatum, the impact creating a loud crash of helmets and pads that echoed throughout the stadium. The ball, caught in the chaos, became an unwilling player in this unfolding drama. It bounced off Fuqua's shoulder, flying up into the air like a rebellious bird breaking free, leaving the fans gasping in disbelief. Time seemed to stretch; those fleeting seconds felt like an eternity as the crowd watched the ball float above, uncertain of where it would land.

And there, amidst the swirling confusion, was Franco Harris—an unsung hero of the play, ready to become a household name. Positioned just right, Harris focused intently on the soaring football, his instincts kicking into high gear. With the elegance of a dancer, he lunged forward, arm outstretched, determination shining on his face. In one seamless motion, he snatched the ball from the air, just inches above the turf, cradling it as if it were the most precious thing in the world.

The moment he made that incredible catch, a deafening roar erupted from the stands, drowning out everything else around him. What started as disbelief turned into wild joy, as the crowd exploded into a chorus of cheers that shook the stadium to its core. With adrenaline rushing through his veins, Harris sprinted toward the end zone, a blur of black and gold. Teammates followed him, fueled by a wave of excitement that felt almost magical.

The energy surged through players and fans alike, creating a beautiful harmony of joy and celebration. As Harris crossed into the end zone, it felt like the sky itself had opened up to shower the Steelers faithful with happiness. After a moment of uncertainty, the referees raised their arms in victory, signaling a touchdown. Harris hadn't just caught a ball; he had caught a piece of history.

Every fan in the stadium, every child watching from home, felt the emotional weight of that moment. In an instant, Franco Harris transformed from a rookie running back into a football legend. The echoes of the crowd, cheering and celebrating, would cement that play in the story of football. Harris became the embodiment of hope, resilience, and the sheer magic of the game, forever altering the landscape of sports.

As the cheers continued to wash over the field, Harris was swept up in the celebration. Teammates surrounded him, lifting him high as they formed a circle around their hero, a bond forged in the heat of competition. Cameras flashed, capturing the jubilation, while announcers searched for words that could possibly do justice to the extraordinary scene. This was more than just a touchdown; it was a moment that declared the Pittsburgh Steelers were no longer just players—they were serious contenders for greatness.

Yet, while the thrill of victory was palpable, the story of the "Immaculate

Reception" reaches beyond the game itself. It carries a deeper message, one that resonates with young athletes and fans everywhere. Franco Harris showed us that sometimes, everything falls into place, and fortune smiles upon those who are ready. His preparation and readiness to seize the moment when it came would inspire generations to come.

In the months and years that followed, the "Immaculate Reception" would be replayed time and again on highlight reels, becoming a source of pride not just for the Steelers organization, but for the entire city of Pittsburgh. It evolved into a cultural milestone, a story parents shared with their children, and kids recounted to friends on playgrounds, igniting dreams of their own glory on the field.

Harris's legacy blossomed, not just as a player, but as a symbol of hope, determination, and the unexpected turns life can take. He became a role model for young athletes, a reminder that regardless of the challenges one faces, greatness is achievable through hard work, dedication, and a willingness to take a chance when the opportunity arises.

As young readers today think about the incredible journey of Franco Harris and that unforgettable play, they are encouraged to nurture the same readiness in their own lives. Whether it's in sports, school, or personal goals, every moment presents an opportunity for greatness, waiting just beneath the surface for someone willing to seize it. The echoes of that day in 1972 continue to inspire, a powerful reminder that sometimes, being in the right place at the right time can lead to remarkable outcomes.

The "Immaculate Reception" is not just a moment in sports history; it's a testament to belief, teamwork, and the wild unpredictability of life. So as we celebrate that remarkable catch, let's remember Franco Harris—not just as a player, but as an inspiration for every aspiring athlete dreaming of their own moment to shine.

Always Stay Alert

When the spotlight is on and everything is at stake, how ready are you to grab that chance? This question hits home in the world of sports, where a single play can change the course of a game, a season, or even a player's career. Franco Harris knew this all too well, and his unforgettable moment during the 1972 playoffs shows just how crucial it is to be prepared for the unexpected.

Think about all the things that come together in a split second: the play call, the quarterback's anticipation, the positioning of teammates, and of course, the unpredictable nature of the ball itself. Although Harris wasn't the star of the play designed by Coach Noll, he stayed alert, standing in the right place at the right time. This level of awareness isn't just luck; it's a skill built on hard work, discipline, and a deep commitment to the game.

In life, much like in football, it's vital to develop a mindset that gets you ready for opportunities. Often, remarkable moments show up disguised as everyday events, just waiting for someone to see their importance. The trick is realizing that every moment has potential. Whether you're taking a test at school, auditioning for a role, or aiming for a game-winning shot, staying alert can be the difference between success and missed opportunities.

Harris's readiness didn't come just from instinct; it was a result of preparation. Athletes put in countless hours of training—practicing drills, studying playbooks, and analyzing their opponents. This hard work not only improves their physical skills but also sharpens their mental focus. When the crucial moment comes, all that preparation pays off. Franco Harris embodied this idea; he was always aware of the game around him, the football, and, more importantly, where he needed to be.

Imagine being in his shoes on that pivotal day. The crowd roared like a wild sea of anticipation, nerves, and hope. Franco stood there, a rookie thrown into a critical moment, yet he remained calm, knowing this was more than just another play. He had trained for this, and the pressure only heightened his concentration. The sound of helmets crashing echoed in the air, but Harris didn't flinch. Instead, he kept his eyes on the ball, ready to react to whatever chaos came his way.

To truly appreciate the brilliance of Harris's catch, it's important to grasp the dynamics of that moment. He wasn't just fixated on the ball; he was also tuned into the energy around him—the movements of his teammates and the intensity of the opposing players. This layered awareness reflects his dedication as an athlete and offers a powerful lesson for everyone, young and old: always stay alert and be ready to act.

In sports, the unexpected is the only certainty. Defenses can shift in a heartbeat, a perfect throw can turn disastrous, and a moment of distraction can cost a team the game. The same goes for life. With all its surprises, life often rewards those who keep their eyes open. A chance encounter can blossom into a lifelong friendship, an unexpected question can ignite a new passion, and a fleeting idea can grow into something incredible.

Being alert also means being open to opportunities that might not seem grand at first. Just like Franco found himself poised to make history with a seemingly routine deflection, individuals in every field should remember that greatness often hides in the ordinary. A lesson learned in school might lead to a groundbreaking discovery later on. A small job or internship can be a stepping stone to a dream career. By nurturing a mindset that welcomes every opportunity, we can shape our own paths to success.

After the "Immaculate Reception," Harris became more than just a celebrated player; he became an inspiration. His readiness to seize that moment sends a message to countless aspiring athletes and individuals: hone your skills and stay engaged in your passions, no matter how far off your goals might seem.

The importance of being prepared goes well beyond the football field. Look at the world of science and innovation; countless breakthroughs come from people who stayed alert and acted on a thought or idea. Thomas Edison, for instance, famously said, "Genius is one percent inspiration and ninety-nine percent perspiration." His dedication to experimenting and unwavering focus helped him seize countless opportunities that ultimately changed the world.

Additionally, being aware can strengthen personal relationships and deepen connections. Think of the times a friend needed support or a family member needed someone to listen. By being in tune with the needs of those around you, you can become a source of strength and encouragement, often right when it matters most.

Franco Harris's legacy reminds us that extraordinary moments can spring up in the most unexpected situations. The ball might not always come your way, but when it does, being ready to act can turn the ordinary into the extraordinary. As we reflect on his unforgettable catch, let it inspire us to build a mindset that values preparation, vigilance, and the constant possibility for greatness in our own lives.

As Harris sprinted into the end zone, it wasn't just the joy of scoring that filled him; it was the culmination of all those hours spent refining his skills and getting ready for the unexpected. The players, the fans, the city of Pittsburgh—all shared in that electrifying moment, a powerful reminder of what it means to seize opportunities when they arise.

This moment in history—the catch, the run, the touchdown—wasn't just about Franco Harris. It symbolized the dream of every young athlete, every ambitious student, every person striving for success. Stay alert, keep your eyes wide open, and remember: you never know when the next opportunity will come knocking. Embrace the unexpected and cultivate readiness, because you might just

create a moment that will be celebrated for
generations.

Creating a Legacy

Every great story leaves a mark, and in
the world of sports, legacies often find a special
place in the hearts of fans and players alike.
The "Immaculate Reception" was more than
just an unforgettable play; it became a shining
symbol of hope, resilience, and determination,
forever changing the fate of the Pittsburgh
Steelers and their iconic running back, Franco
Harris. This tale goes beyond the football field
and speaks to anyone who has dared to dream
or faced a tough challenge.

On that memorable day in December
1972, when Harris made a jaw-dropping catch

from a deflected pass and dashed into the end zone, he did far more than score a touchdown. He sparked a passion within a franchise that had long struggled to find its footing. That moment filled the city of Pittsburgh with excitement, spreading through locker rooms, neighborhoods, and the hearts of fans who had long clung to the hope of a brighter future. For many, it represented the power of never giving up and the belief that success is always within reach for those who refuse to back down.

As the Steelers pushed through the rest of the 1972 season, it became clear that the "Immaculate Reception" was just the start of something much bigger than a single game. The victory over the Oakland Raiders led to a playoff run that ultimately brought the franchise to its first Super Bowl appearance. The energy and belief sparked by that incredible moment transformed the Steelers from a struggling team into a powerhouse. They were no longer just another name in the NFL; they became a symbol of grit and determination, embodied by Harris himself.

In Super Bowl IX, where they faced the Minnesota Vikings, Harris was once again in the spotlight. The Steelers clinched their first championship with a strong 16-6 victory, and Harris shined as a key player, rushing for a then-Super Bowl record of 158 yards and scoring a touchdown. With that performance, he became a household name. Kids in Pittsburgh proudly wore his jersey, while fans across the nation began to recognize him as one of the brightest stars in the game. He wasn't just a running back; he was a living legend, and the "Immaculate Reception" was the moment that launched him into football greatness.

The impact of Harris's legendary play stretched far beyond the football field. It inspired countless young athletes. Those who followed his journey learned an important lesson: greatness can emerge from the most unexpected moments. The challenges Harris faced—being a rookie under intense pressure, defying the odds, and seizing the day—are lessons that apply to all of life. They encourage young readers to keep moving forward, even when the odds seem stacked against them.

Think about the future generations of athletes who found inspiration in Harris's legacy. Picture young football players tying their cleats in their backyards, mimicking the moves of their hero and imagining themselves making that game-winning catch, running with the same fierce determination that Harris showed. Coaches began to incorporate his story into their practices, using it as a motivational tool to instill a sense of purpose and resilience in their players. In classrooms, teachers referenced Harris as an example of hard work and dedication, encouraging students to prepare for their own moments of brilliance, however they may show up.

Beyond the world of sports, Harris's influence on popular culture is undeniable. He became a well-known figure on television, appearing on talk shows and in commercials, sharing his story and captivating audiences with his humility and charm. He became a role model for many, demonstrating that success is about more than just talent; it's also about character. The lessons learned from his journey continue to resonate, inspiring young people to rise to the occasion and make their own mark in the world.

Franco Harris's legacy serves as a reflection of the hopes and dreams of countless individuals. It encourages everyone to think about the stories they are creating in their own lives. What moments define who they are? What actions will leave an impression on those around them? Each of us has the power to create a legacy, whether through small acts of kindness, commitment to a cause, or following a passion. The key is to stay aware of the opportunities that come our way, just as Harris did that day on the field.

As young readers think about their own legacies, it's vital to remember that it's not just about making headlines or becoming famous. True legacy is built on the relationships we cultivate, the impact we have on others, and the lessons we share along the way. It's about the friendships formed through competition, the guidance offered to others, and the lasting impression left on the community. The legacy of the "Immaculate Reception" reminds us that every moment, no matter how big or small, can contribute to a larger story—one that transcends the individual and encourages collective growth.

When reflecting on Franco Harris's legendary play and what followed, the message is clear: greatness is attainable for anyone willing to work hard, stay prepared, and keep their eyes open for the opportunities life offers. Just like Harris, who stood ready when the ball deflected off a Raiders player, young readers can develop a mindset that welcomes challenges and embraces the unknown.

In the grand scheme of things, life is a collection of moments, many of which hold the potential for greatness. Every interaction, every choice, and every effort shapes the legacy we build. The challenge lies in spotting these opportunities and responding with courage and determination.

Franco Harris embodied this spirit, and his story encourages us all to look deeper. The "Immaculate Reception" wasn't just an impressive athletic feat; it was a defining moment in history that sparked a legacy grounded in hope, determination, and resilience. For every young person learning about his journey, the message is straightforward: prepare yourself for your moment. You never know when life will throw an unexpected opportunity your way.

So, as you lace up your shoes, whether on the field, in the classroom, or anywhere else, remember the legacy you are crafting. Embrace your dreams, work tirelessly, and, most importantly, stay alert for those defining moments. Just like Franco Harris, you may find that with a little preparation and a lot of heart, you too can seize your extraordinary opportunity and inspire generations to come. The story of the "Immaculate Reception" is just the beginning—your story is waiting to be written.

Chapter 10: Doug Flutie's Hail Mary Magic

Defying Expectations

In the small town of Natick, Massachusetts, a young boy with dreams bigger than his size wandered the football fields. Doug Flutie was far from the typical quarterback—he didn't tower over the defensive linemen like the others. Standing at just 5 feet 10 inches, Doug was a pocket of determination in a world that often prioritized size over skill. Yet it was this very courage and unyielding spirit that would define his football career and life.

Doug faced more than just physical challenges as a child; he also dealt with the doubts of those around him. Coaches at his high school looked at his height with skepticism, often questioning whether someone his size could ever lead a team to victory. They fell into the trap of believing that sheer size was the only measure of a player's potential. Little did they know, they had a diamond in the rough in Doug—a player whose skills would shine bright even in the darkest moments of doubt.

From the moment he first threw a football, Doug's passion was undeniable. He would spend hours tossing that ball against the side of his house, the rhythmic thud of leather against wood echoing his determination. Every pass he completed added a little more confidence, building a belief that he could break down the barriers in front of him. He practiced each throw meticulously, developing not just his technique, but also a deep understanding of the game that belied his age.

His childhood was filled with moments that would later become pivotal in his journey. He recalled a day at a local park when he spotted a group of older boys tossing a football back and forth, flaunting their strength. Doug approached them, asking if he could join in. They laughed at him, dismissing him with mocking chuckles. Undeterred, Doug picked up the ball, launched it into the air with surprising accuracy, and watched it spiral beautifully through the sky. The boys were stunned. "Whoa! Where'd you learn to throw like that?" one of them asked. Just like that, Doug Flutie began to create a new identity— one built on talent, not limitations.

Throughout high school, Doug worked hard to improve his skills. Every summer, you could find him at the local field, throwing passes to anyone who would catch. He learned to make up for his lack of height with quick thinking, impressive footwork, and an uncanny ability to read defenses. His friends and teammates began to recognize his extraordinary talent. They admired his relentless pursuit of excellence, and slowly, the whispers of doubt faded away. The boy who once seemed insignificant was now a name whispered with respect.

Flutie's determination caught the eye of his high school coach, who eventually saw his potential. With the coach's encouragement, Doug stepped up to lead the team. Each game became an opportunity for him to show that he was more than just a player defined by his height. He led with heart and determination, turning skeptics into supporters. Fans filled the stands, rallying behind the underdog with a loyalty that spoke volumes about Doug's character.

But the road to success wasn't always smooth. There were games where he struggled, moments of self-doubt, and nights when he wondered if he would ever find his place in a sport that seemed to favor giants. Yet, each challenge only fueled his resolve. In those tough moments, Doug discovered the true meaning of resilience. Every setback became a stepping stone, pushing him to work even harder and keep striving for greatness.

As he moved on to college, Doug found himself at Boston College, where the stakes were higher and the competition fiercer. But instead of feeling overwhelmed, he thrived. He quickly made a name for himself as a star quarterback, proving time and again that success isn't about height; it's about the heart and passion inside. His college career was filled with unforgettable moments, but none was more defining than the game against Miami in 1984—a match that would solidify his legacy.

As the clock ticked down, Boston College was trailing and faced with what seemed like impossible odds. The crowd held its breath, and even the most die-hard fans couldn't help but feel anxious. But Doug stayed calm and focused, his mind clear as he took control of the huddle. The play was called, and as the ball was snapped, Flutie launched a desperate throw towards the end zone—an instant that would be remembered in football history.

The ball soared above the defenders, creating a beautiful arc that seemed to defy gravity, as if lifted by the dreams of every underdog who ever dared to chase their aspirations. Time seemed to slow, and for what felt like an eternity, everyone's eyes were glued to that ball. When it was finally caught in the end zone, the stadium erupted into chaos, a mix of cheers and disbelief. Doug Flutie had not only led his team to victory; he had shattered every expectation placed upon him.

That moment wasn't just about winning a game; it was a testament to his journey and a reminder that hard work, belief, and unyielding determination can overcome even the toughest challenges. It struck a chord with everyone who had ever felt small in the face of adversity. Doug's story became a symbol of hope, reminding us all that we shouldn't let other people's perceptions limit our potential. He stood for young athletes everywhere, showing that greatness isn't defined by size, but by the courage to rise above doubt.

As young readers take in Doug Flutie's journey from a determined boy in Natick to a celebrated quarterback, they learn that perseverance is what binds together the stories of extraordinary athletes. Doug's tale shows us that every throw, every tackle, and every moment of doubt is part of a bigger story—one that inspires all of us to chase our dreams with passion and heart. The lessons from his early years echo through the highs and lows of his career, highlighting the truth that believing in oneself can unlock doors that once seemed closed. In a world that often measures success by stature, Doug Flutie proved that sometimes, the heart of a champion beats strongest in the most unlikely of bodies.

The Unforgettable Throw

The sun was setting over the Boston College campus on that memorable November afternoon in 1984, painting the sky with a warm golden glow. The stadium buzzed with excitement, filled with fans whose energy electrified the air as they anticipated the big game against the Miami Hurricanes. Doug Flutie stood at the edge of the huddle, his heart racing along with the crowd. This was more than just another game; it was a moment that would go down in history. The tension in the stadium was thick, as if time itself was bending under the pressure of everyone's expectations.

As the clock ticked away, Boston College was behind, and the scoreboard reflected the uphill battle they faced. Cheers from Miami supporters echoed ominously across the field, while Boston College fans held their breath, their hopes teetering on the edge. It was a high-pressure moment—one that could challenge even the toughest athletes. But Doug was no ordinary player; he was a fighter, a quarterback who had spent his life proving that the size of a person's heart could surpass the limitations of his height.

"Alright, listen up!" Doug shouted, gathering his teammates' attention, his voice steady amidst the swirling chaos. "We've got one shot at this. We've worked too hard to let it slip away now." His teammates nodded, soaking in his unshakeable confidence, a belief that would soon serve as their lifeline as they geared up for a play that could lead to either triumph or heartbreak.

The atmosphere crackled with energy as the players lined up, the roar of the crowd fading into a distant hum compared to the thunderous beat of Doug's heart. He took a deep breath, centering himself in the moment. This wasn't just about winning the game; it was the culmination of all the challenges he had faced—the skeptics, the critics, the doubts tied to his height. This was his chance to show that nothing was out of reach.

The snap echoed through the field, sharp and clear. Doug's feet were firmly planted in the pocket as he scanned the field like a hawk searching for its prey. He felt the pressure of the defense closing in, but he stood his ground, determined. As he assessed his options, time seemed to stretch. In the midst of the chaos, he felt a calmness, a clarity that came from his unwavering resolve.

Then, like a bolt of lightning, he spotted his target—a receiver sprinting down the sideline, fingers twitching with excitement. Doug's mind was crystal clear. He had practiced this throw countless times in his backyard, imagining moments like this— moments that went beyond the game. With a flick of his wrist, he launched the ball into the air.

The ball soared upward, gliding gracefully against the backdrop of the setting sun. In that fleeting moment, it felt like the entire stadium was holding its breath, the hopes of thousands hanging on the outcome. Doug watched in slow motion as the ball arced beautifully through the sky, defying gravity like a dream come to life. It was a Hail Mary pass, a desperate throw filled with equal parts faith and determination. He envisioned it flying like a comet, shining bright with the weight of his dreams.

As the ball sailed, the world around him faded away. For the players on the field, the fans in the stands, and even the commentators, time seemed to stand still. Every eye was on the ball, every heart raced with the thrill of the moment. Defenders leaped, arms stretched wide, but they seemed like mere shadows compared to Doug's vision. He knew this throw could change everything.

Then, in an instant, it all came together. The receiver's hands reached out, fingers brushing the leather of the ball, just a heartbeat away from glory. In a flash, he caught it firmly, as if plucking a star from the sky. The crowd erupted—a thunderous roar that shattered the tension like glass. Cheering, gasping, and shouting in disbelief, the fans were swept up in a wave of joy. Doug had done it. He had turned the impossible into reality.

In the end zone, the receiver fell to his knees, cradling the ball in triumph. The stadium exploded in a mix of joy and disbelief, a celebration that went beyond the realm of sports. Doug was engulfed by his teammates, their shouts of victory blending with the crowd's deafening cheers. He had made his mark, not just on that game but in the hearts of everyone watching. The Hail Mary pass wasn't just a moment of brilliance; it was a powerful reminder of the strength of dreams and the determination to make them come true.

The impact of that unforgettable throw reached far beyond the football field. It echoed in the hearts of young athletes everywhere, encouraging them to chase after their own Hail Mary moments. For Doug Flutie, that moment defined who he was. It showcased not just his talent as a quarterback but the spirit of resilience he had built over the years. It served as proof that greatness often arises from hardship and that the heart of a champion knows no limits.

As the excitement settled from that thrilling day, Doug realized that the road ahead would still be filled with challenges. But he had crossed a crucial threshold. The boy from Natick, who once faced doubt, now stood tall, embraced by the love of fans who saw in him a reflection of their own aspirations. He had become a beacon of hope, inspiring those who dared to dream, showing that extraordinary moments can come from the most unexpected places.

And so, Doug Flutie's story would always be linked to that legendary throw—a moment forever etched in football history, reminding us that when time is running out, all you need is a little faith, a whole lot of heart, and maybe, just maybe, a Hail Mary to change everything.

Believing in Yourself

Life can be a lot like a football game—full of surprises, twists, and moments that feel too tough to overcome. Doug Flutie's story is a great example of how believing in yourself can lead to incredible accomplishments. He went from being overlooked to shining bright in the spotlight, showing us how important it is to have confidence and to follow our dreams.

So, how can young athletes and dreamers build that self-belief? Gaining confidence isn't always a straight line; it's often a winding road with its share of bumps and unexpected turns. The first step is recognizing that everyone has doubts. Even star athletes like Doug have faced skepticism. It's important to realize that doubt is part of the journey, and having faith in yourself can light the way through tough times.

Start by embracing what makes you unique. Just as Doug's height made him stand out, our differences are what set us apart. Think about what makes you who you are—your interests, your style, and your passions.

Instead of trying to fit into someone else's idea of normal, celebrate your individuality. This celebration can spark a newfound self-belief that pushes you forward. Doug didn't fit the typical mold of a quarterback; he embraced his height and proved that greatness can come in all forms.

Next, take some risks. Stepping out of your comfort zone is where amazing things can happen. Remember that famous Hail Mary pass? Doug didn't just wait for opportunities; he went for it. Each time you try something new—like switching positions on the field, joining a competition, or even asking a question in class—you're stretching your comfort zone. Welcome those chances; they might lead to unexpected experiences that boost your confidence.

Set achievable goals for yourself. Breaking down bigger dreams into smaller, easier steps can make your journey feel less overwhelming. If you aspire to be a star athlete, start with daily practice, focus on improving your skills, and keep track of your progress. Celebrate every little victory, whether it's mastering a new technique, hitting a personal best, or just showing up to practice. Each small step reinforces your belief in yourself and reminds you of what you can achieve.

Engagement is also crucial. Surround yourself with people who lift you up and encourage you. Just like Doug had teammates who believed in him, you should find friends, family, coaches, and mentors who inspire you. Their faith in your abilities can boost your self-confidence and keep you motivated, especially during tough times. When life gets heavy, kind words from those who care can give you the lift you need to keep pushing forward.

It's also important to build resilience. Life will throw challenges your way; that's part of the game. How you handle setbacks can shape your journey. Doug faced plenty of criticism throughout his career, but he didn't let it bring him down; instead, he used it as motivation. When you encounter obstacles, ask yourself what you can learn from them. Turn challenges into stepping stones rather than stumbling blocks. Resilience isn't about never falling; it's about getting back up every time you do.

As you chase your dreams, visualize your success. Close your eyes and picture yourself achieving your goals. Imagine the thrill, the excitement when you accomplish what once seemed impossible. Visualization can help create a strong connection between your mind and body, getting you ready to take the steps needed to make those dreams a reality. Just like athletes rehearse their plays, you can envision your own successes.

Ask yourself some thought-provoking questions to keep your passion alive. What would you try if you knew you couldn't fail? What dreams have you put aside because of fear? These questions can uncover hidden desires and remind you of your potential. Let them drive you to take action. Whether it's picking up a football and practicing every day or dedicating time to learn something you love, let those dreams simmer and then rise to the surface.

Practice gratitude while you work toward your goals. Recognizing the good things in your life can change your perspective and strengthen your belief in yourself. Each little success—like a compliment from a coach, a nod from a friend, or personal progress—deserves acknowledgment. Keep a journal of your achievements, big and small, and look back at it whenever self-doubt sneaks in. It's a wonderful reminder of how far you've come and all the moments that have shaped your path.

Remember, failure is part of the journey to growth. Doug Flutie didn't always succeed on the field; he faced many challenges and disappointments. But those setbacks became crucial lessons that helped mold him into the player he was. Embrace failures as chances to learn instead of signs of weakness. The greatest athletes know that every setback is just a setup for a comeback.

As you work on building self-belief, remember that perseverance is key. Success usually doesn't happen overnight. It takes hard work, dedication, and the willingness to push through the tough moments. Create a routine that aligns with your goals and stick to it, even when motivation fades. Surround yourself with inspiration—put up quotes that resonate with you on your wall, or create a vision board that showcases your dreams. The more you fill your life with positivity and determination, the stronger you'll become.

In the end, believing in yourself isn't about being perfect; it's about understanding your value and potential, just like Doug Flutie did. Embrace your journey, with all its ups and downs. When self-doubt creeps in, remember Doug's story—a tale of courage, determination, and the life-changing power of self-belief. Let it guide you forward, knowing that greatness is within each of you, waiting to be unlocked.

So, what are you waiting for? Go out there, trust in yourself, and dream big. Whether you're on the football field, in school, or facing personal challenges, remember that self-belief is your greatest ally. Just like Doug Flutie, you have the ability to turn the impossible into possible. The only

limits are the ones you set for yourself, and it's
time to break free and soar to new heights.
Your dreams are out there, and it's time to
chase them with the heart of a champion.

References

Chapter 1:
Tom Brady | Biography, Accomplishments, Statistics, &
Facts: https://www.britannica.com/biography/Tom-Brady

Tom Brady -
Wikipedia: https://en.wikipedia.org/wiki/Tom_Brady

Tom Brady is the greatest underdog story in American sports
history: https://sports.yahoo.com/tom-brady-is-the-greatest-underdog-story-in-american-sports-history-period-160830589.html

Chapter 2:
Kurt Warner | Biography &
Facts: https://www.britannica.com/biography/Kurt-Warner

Kurt Warner -
Wikipedia: https://en.wikipedia.org/wiki/Kurt_Warner

Kurt Warner | Pro Football Hall of
Fame: https://www.profootballhof.com/players/kurt-warner/

Chapter 3:

Jerry Rice Biography: NFL Football Player - Ducksters: https://www.ducksters.com/sports/jerry_rice.php

The Official Site of Jerry Rice | About: https://www.jerryricefootball.com/about

Jerry Rice shared a story about his work ethic: https://www.aol.com/article/2015/09/15/jerry-rice-story-about-how-he-got-his-work-ethic-is-awesome/21236395/

Chapter 4:

Brett Favre - Wikipedia: https://en.wikipedia.org/wiki/Brett_Favre

Brett Favre | Biography & Facts: https://www.britannica.com/biography/Brett-Favre

Brett Favre | Pro Football Hall of Fame: https://www.profootballhof.com/players/brett-favre/

Chapter 5:

Walter Payton - Stats, Death & Career - Biography: https://www.biography.com/athlete/walter-payton

Walter Payton - Wikipedia: https://en.wikipedia.org/wiki/Walter_Payton

Walter Payton | Pro Football Hall of Fame: https://www.profootballhof.com/players/walter-payton/

Chapter 6:
David Tyree - Wikipedia: https://en.wikipedia.org/wiki/David_Tyree

The story behind David Tyree's legendary 'Helmet Catch': https://www.nfl.com/news/the-story-behind-david-tyree-s-legendary-helmet-catch-0ap3000000910410

David Tyree's Super Bowl XLII helmet catch: https://www.giants.com/video/david-tyree-s-super-bowl-xlii-helmet-catch-2493597

Chapter 7:
Joe Montana | Biography, Stats, & Facts: https://www.britannica.com/biography/Joe-Montana

Joe Montana - Wikipedia: https://en.wikipedia.org/wiki/Joe_Montana

Joe Montana | Pro Football Hall of
Fame: https://www.profootballhof.com/players
/joe-montana/

Chapter 8:
Marshawn Lynch -
Wikipedia: https://en.wikipedia.org/wiki/Mars
hawn_Lynch

Marshawn Lynch | Biography &
Facts: https://www.britannica.com/biography/
Marshawn-Lynch

Marshawn Lynch Career
Highlights: https://www.nfl.com/videos/marsha
wn-lynch-career-highlights

Chapter 9:
Franco Harris -
Wikipedia: https://en.wikipedia.org/wiki/Fran
co_Harris

Franco Harris | Biography &
Facts: https://www.britannica.com/biography/F
ranco-Harris

The Immaculate Reception | Pro Football
Hall of
Fame: https://www.profootballhof.com/footbal
l-history/the-immaculate-reception/

Chapter 10:

Doug Flutie -
Wikipedia: https://en.wikipedia.org/wiki/Doug
_Flutie

Doug Flutie's Hail Mary: The Pass That
Launched a
Legend: https://www.si.com/college/2019/11/2
1/doug-flutie-hail-mary-boston-college-miami

Doug Flutie | Pro Football Hall of
Fame: https://www.profootballhof.com/players
/doug-flutie/

W. Bo Cricklewood